Twayne's United States Authors Series

EDITOR OF THIS VOLUME

Warren French

Indiana University

Amiri Baraka

TUSAS 383

AMIRI BARAKA

By LLOYD W. BROWN
University of Southern California

TWAYNE PUBLISHERS

A DIVISION OF G. K. HALL & CO., BOSTON

Library of Congress Cataloging in Publication Data

Brown, Lloyd W
Amiri Baraka.

(Twayne's United States authors series ; TUSAS
383)
Bibliography: p. 173–78
Includes index.
1.   Baraka, Imamu Amiri, 1934–   —Criticism
and interpretation.
PS3552.A583Z57   818'.5409   80–22990
ISBN 0–8057–7317–7

Contents

About the Author

Lloyd W. Brown is Jamaican born, received his degrees from the University of the West Indies and the University of Toronto, and is now Professor of Comparative Literature at the University of Southern California. His primary interests of research and teaching are black literature, women writers, and the novel, and he has published extensively in these areas. His major publications include *Bits of Ivory: Narrative Techniques in Jane Austen's Fiction* (1973), *The Black Writer in Africa and the Americas* (1973), and *West Indian Poetry* (1978).

Preface

Amiri Baraka, born Everett LeRoi Jones, has been a controversial figure in American politics and literature for the last sixteen years. As a brilliant young poet and fresh, provocative dramatist he was lionized by the literary establishment of the mid-1960s, winning two distinguished fellowships and an Obie drama award by his thirtieth year, and generally compelling attention, even from hostile critics, as a major new talent in black American literature and in American literature as a whole. During the racial turbulence that followed those earlier years Baraka's political activism earned him additional attention, climaxed by his national visibility as one of the major leaders of the national black convention in Atlanta in 1970. And while his poetry, drama, and political activism continue to make him a significant figure in black America, his work as art critic represents an important contribution to the debates of the 1960s and early 1970s. Consequently he has become one of the leading representatives of what is now known as the black aesthetic, or black arts movement, which still seeks to define the alleged peculiarities of the black American's art and art criticism.

But, curiously, for some time serious study of Baraka's work lagged far behind his undoubted achievements and his undeniable reputation. This neglect can be traced, in part, to the fact that Baraka's work has frequently attracted political reaction, or more precisely, political invective, rather than informed and informative analysis. In one sense this kind of reaction is understandable, even inevitable, though not really excusable for all that. Baraka's visibility as black political activist and his frank insistence on the political significance of his literary art have usually aroused unease about his racial militancy, and have encouraged the assumption that his work is political propaganda rather than "serious" art.

However, this kind of assumption has not been very helpful. Although Baraka has been adamant about his political role and vision he has never ceased to produce works that are recognizably distinct from the pamphlets, essays, and speeches that comprise direct political statement. Although he attacks the usual academic insistence on art for its own sake, Baraka clearly makes a distinction between art, even politically committed art, and the tracts, speeches, and other tools of his political activism. Otherwise it would be difficult to account for the fact that during his most politically committed periods he has continued to write as poet and dramatist. In the process he has obviously continued to invite study as a writer whose political activism is integrated with his art (at least on his own terms). And his continuing interest in the creation of literary art forms—albeit fervently committed art forms—implies more than political commitment as such. It also represents a continuing and deep-rooted interest in all of those definable constructs and indeterminate traits which are peculiar to art, whether art is viewed as a self-contained, self-justifying mode or seen as an integral part of a political process. Unfortunately for the student of Baraka the political responses to Baraka the activist have resulted in the neglect of Baraka the artist, and have therefore distorted the achievements and the reciprocity of both.

This neglect has not been total, of course. But the serious critical attention has been uneven. Much of the focus has been on the earlier plays, especially on *Dutchman*, which on a purely statistical basis accounts for the bulk of extant Baraka criticism. This unevenness stems in part from the frequent claim that after 1964 (the date of *Dutchman*) Baraka's art gave way to mere political invective. It is also due to a certain uneasiness with Baraka's development as writer and thinker. There is a suspicion which surfaces occasionally that there is something unstable (and therefore unworthy of serious scholarly attention) in an intellectual evolution that has brought Baraka from the "Beat" generation of Greenwich Village poets, through the period of black nationalism, to the more recent conversion to Marxist-Leninism.[1]

Since 1973, however, some significant changes have been taking place in Baraka scholarship. The passing of the earlier political confrontations seems to have left more room for the kind of reasonable, investigative criticism that is exemplified by several scholarly papers on selected aspects of Baraka's work. The upsurge of serious scholarly interest has coincided with the appearance of three book-length studies—Theodore Hudson's *From LeRoi Jones to Amiri Baraka* (1973), Kimberly Benston's *The Renegade and the Mask* (1976), and Werner Sollors's *Amiri Baraka/LeRoi Jones: The Quest for a "Populist Modernism"* (1978). Hudson's work is particularly helpful in the area of Baraka's biography; Benston examines aspects of Baraka's intellectual development; and Sollors examines Baraka's literary career as the reflection of his ideological development.

In effect, the recent criticism has helped to generate an atmosphere in which interest in Baraka's art can grow. At the same time the relatively specialist nature of most of these better studies has left room for a fairly comprehensive analysis, one that surveys Baraka's achievements in the various genres represented by his writings as a whole. The generic approach to Baraka's work in this study is more than a matter of stressing forms for their own sake. Given Baraka's insistence on the thematic function of form, then the writer's very choice of genres assumes a certain significance in his work. Each of Baraka's genres—essay, novel, short story, poetry, and drama—reflects certain aspects of his development as politically committed writer, and it simultaneously helps to define the very nature of the experience which it contains. Thus the essays are the direct statements of the political activist and critic. That directness clarifies the relationship between Baraka's personal development and his political ideas. Moreover the special role of the expository essays underlines Baraka's clear distinction between his interest in the written word as committed art and his use of unadorned political statement.

The prose fiction is distinct in Baraka's work, not only as a genre, but also as a form which he abandons relatively early in his career. This abandonment is significant, particularly in view of Baraka's personal view of prose fiction as an inherently white, Western mode. Precisely because of its "alien" cultural sources, Baraka's prose fiction is peculiarly suited to the central themes of his novel (*The System of Dante's Hell*) and his short stories (*Tales*)—the conflict between an "alien" white value system and black identity. This cultural conflict is perversely appropriate for a fictive form since Baraka is always able to dramatize the struggle by continuously striking out at the form itself. Narrative patterns in these works arise, paradoxically, from a violent assault on preconceived notions of fictive form and on the (white, Western) culture that is the source of those notions.

Baraka's dual perception of form and language—both as form of communication and target of attack—runs throughout the poetry. Here, in a genre which spans most of Baraka's career as writer, form and structure have evolved to cohere with his themes in a direct way, rather than by virtue of the paradoxical ironies of the prose fiction. Poetry allows Baraka an unparalleled latitude, accommodating his need to destroy forms, create new structures, and to exploit language itself while demonstrating its limitations. And part of this accomplishment rests in the fact that Baraka's use of black folk forms (music and language, for example) invests his poetry with an "ethnic" legitimacy that the "alien" forms of prose fiction seem to lack in his view.

But in spite of the relatively consistent successes of the poetry it is the drama that most seems to attract Baraka. This fascination lies in his perception of art as commitment and in the peculiar identity of drama itself. As both word and action the form has a special appeal to the political activist who requires, even demands, an artistic mode that is distinct from but complementary to straightforward political activism. This probably explains why, as Baraka's personal activism has intensified and broadened, he has turned more and more to the stage. For example, his most significant work as a convert to socialism has been in drama—*The Motion of History* (1976) and *S-1* (1976).

As a result the drama reflects much of Baraka's recent growth as a writer. But for a similar reason his plays comprise his most uneven achievements, ranging from the penetrating insights of *Dutchman* and *The Slave* to the unimaginative baldness of later pieces where committed art seems to have degenerated into a mere preachiness. But even here it is necessary to distinguish between the failures as such and that interest in artistic form which is still implicit even in the most palpable failures. Either as the black nationalist producer of street theater, or as the writer of drama as scientific socialism, Baraka is self-consciously the artist seeking to integrate his political views of the moment with distinctive art forms. Hence even at its worst Baraka's drama demands attention, not simply as political statement but as politically involved art. This is also true of his work as a whole, and the present study attempts to respond to that demand by exploring facets of his achievement in each of his chosen genres.

On the whole all the important features of Baraka's development as committed artist are amply demonstrated by his major collections. Consequently this study will not dwell on the formidable number of uncollected poems, short stories and essays which Baraka has written. By a similar token the poetry collection, *Hard Facts*, is a body of flimsy poems that are of little value in the understanding of Baraka as socialist writer—certainly less valuable in this regard than his socialist drama. Moreover, the study of the drama will concentrate on the published works, omitting pieces which have been rarely performed but which are otherwise inaccessible to the general public. And as in the case of *Hard Facts*, it has been logical and convenient to omit

these works since they do not add significantly to an understanding of
Baraka's work.

A final note: the study refers throughout the text to the author as
Amiri Baraka since this is the name by which he prefers to be known
and since this allows for consistency. However, in order to avoid
confusion the footnotes and bibliography refer to each title by the
name under which it was originally published—for example, LeRoi
Jones, *Dead Lecturer*, but Amiri Baraka, *Spirit Reach*.

LLOYD W. BROWN

University of Southern California, Los Angeles

Acknowledgments

This study includes materials previously published in *Black American Literature Forum* (formerly *Negro American Literature Forum*), *Journal of Ethnic Studies*, *Journal of Popular Culture*, and *Obsidian*. The permission of the editors to reprint is gratefully acknowledged.

Chronology

1934   Amiri Baraka born as Everett LeRoi Jones on October 7, in Newark, New Jersey.

1940–   Early education at Central Avenue Elementary School and
1951   Barringer High School, Newark.

1951–   Attends Rutgers University on scholarship.
1952

1952   Transfers to Howard University.

1954   Graduates with the Bachelor of Arts degree from Howard University. Undertakes some graduate research at the New School for Social Research.

1954–   Serves in the United States Air Force, reaching rank of
1957   sergeant at the Strategic Air Command posts in Puerto Rico and Germany.

1958   Settles in Greenwich Village where he joins the so-called "Beat Generation" of poets and where his circle includes poets Allen Ginsberg and Charles Olson, avant-garde musicians and playwrights. Marries Hettie Cohen on October 13. The marriage eventually produces two children, Lisa and Kellie.

1958–   Cofounder and coeditor (with Hettie Cohen) of *Yugen*, a
1963   literary magazine.

1959   Compiler of pro-Castro anthology, *Fidel Castro*.

1960   Visits Cuba, together with other black American writers, as guest of Fidel Castro's revolutionary government.

1960–   Awarded Whitney Fellowship.
1961

1960–   Active as editor of new poetry at Totem Press.
1963

1961   Edits *Four Young Lady Poets*. Publishes first collection of poems, *Preface to a Twenty Volume Suicide Note*. Founds, with Diane Di Prima, the American Theatre for Poets, an experimental poetry group. They also launch *The Floating Bear*, an underground magazine supporting new poets.

1963   Edits *The Moderns*, completes first major play, *The Toilet*, and publishes his study of black music in America, *Blues People*.

1963–   Teaches courses in contemporary poetry and in creative writ-
1965   ing at the New School for Social Research.

1964   Produces *Dutchman* and *The Slave*. His second collection of poetry, *The Dead Lecturer*, is published. Wins Obie award for off-Broadway production of *Dutchman*. Teaches summer course in modern poetry at the University of Buffalo.

1965   Publishes his only novel, *The System of Dante's Hell*. Receives Yoruba Academy Fellowship. Divorces Hettie Cohen, then leaves Greenwich Village and the "Beat" circle for Harlem. After directing the shortlived Black Arts Repertory Theater School in Harlem, he moves to Newark where he organizes Spirit House, a black community and arts center.

1965–   Guggenheim Fellowship.
1966

1966   *Baptism* and *Home: Social Essays* are published. *The Slave* receives second prize at the International Arts Festival, Dakar. National Endowment for the Arts grant. Marries Sylvia Robinson in August.

1966–   Visiting lecturer, San Francisco State College. Comes under
1967   the influence of West Coast black nationalist, Ron Karenga, founder and leader of the black nationalist organization, US.

1967   Forms local community group, United Brothers of Newark. He is arrested, during Newark riots of July, on charges of unlawfully carrying firearms and resisting arrest. Subsequent conviction is reversed on appeal. Founds Jihad Publications in order to support black nationalist artists. *Arm Yourself or Harm Yourself* is produced. *Tales*, his only collection of short stories, appears. Screenplay version of *Dutchman. Black Music* is published.

1968   Joins Committee for Unified Newark. Forms Black Community Development and Defense Organization, and launches a political program of black nationalism that is aimed at achieving local black power through Newark's electoral machinery. *Home on the Range* and *Police* are published. Coedits (with Larry Neal) *Black Fire*, an anthology of young black writers.

1969   *Black Magic: Collected Poetry, The Death of Malcolm X*, and *Four Black Revolutionary Plays* are published. Edits *The Cricket* (on black music).

1970   Mobilizes support for successful non-white political candidates in Newark's municipal elections. A major organizer of the Congress of African People, Atlanta. *In Our Terribleness, It's Nation Time, Jello* are published.

1971   *Bloodrites, Junkies Are Full of SHHH . . . , Raise Race Rays Raze.*

1972   *Ba-Ra-Ka, Black Power Chant* join Baraka's growing list of black nationalist agit prop plays. *Kawaida Studies* and *Spirit Reach*. Edits *Congress of African Peoples* (based on 1970 Atlanta conference).

1975   Explains his shift from black nationalism to socialism in *Black World* article (July), "Why I changed My Ideology." *Hard Facts*, a collection of socialist poems.

1977–
1978   Visiting lecturer in black literature, Yale University.

1978   *The Motion of History and Other Plays.*

CHAPTER 1

LeRoi Jones/Amiri Baraka

I The Rebellion of LeRoi Jones

B ARAKA'S career as political activist has made him one of America's most public of contemporary writers. Particularly in the 1960s and early 1970s, he was prominent in mass media reports as one of the more articulate spokesmen of the militant wing of the black civil rights movement. And indeed this political prominence has often tended, in some quarters, to obscure the substance of his achievement as a writer. On the other hand, the integration of his activism and his literary art requires that the student of his writings be familiar with at least the broad outlines of his personal life—a requirement that tends to be more crucial in Baraka's case than with many other writers of comparable stature.

Very little in Baraka's background foreshadows the subsequent notoriety of the radical activist or the impact of the writer. He was born as Everett LeRoi Jones in Newark, New Jersey, on October 7, 1934. His family was comparable with countless lower middle-class families in black America, with the parents earning a modest living as government workers and living in a predominantly black urban community: the mother, Anna Lois Jones, was a social welfare worker and the father, Coyt LeRoy Jones, was a postal worker. Baraka's own childhood was likewise unremarkable, except for a surprisingly early fascination with political speeches by historical figures. And it is known that he tried to write short fiction in high school.

He was apparently an academically gifted student in high school since he received several scholarship offers when he graduated. He accepted an offer from Rutgers University, where he enrolled in 1951. His freshman year at Rutgers was also his last. He never felt comfortable with the social atmosphere there, largely, it seems, because he felt like the black outsider in a predominantly white world. In his sophomore year he transferred to Howard University, from which he eventually graduated with a Bachelor of Arts degree in 1954.

But he was not satisfied with the social life at Howard University. For some years now it has been the custom to cite a notorious incident in which he allegedly ran afoul of university officials for eating a watermelon on the campus. Theodore Hudson, for one, has pointed out that even Baraka's own account of the affair leaves some doubt as to what actually happened.[1] But apocryphal or not, the incident does dramatize that uneasiness with Howard's black middle-class milieu which Baraka was to attack repeatedly in his essays and short stories.

On the whole his experience as university student had a significant bearing on the development of his social consciousness. In many respects his discomfort with the predominantly white campus at Rutgers was not all that different from the experience of countless other blacks whose prevarsity lives offered minimal contacts with whites. But given Baraka's early interest in political issues, it is not surprising that the sense of cultural isolation at Rutgers left a deep impression. In turn that sense of isolation sparked a hunger for a racially compatible and culturally stimulating environment—the very hunger that eventually made Howard inadequate in his eyes, because the university seemed to be too much devoted to the business of black middle-class achievement on the terms of the white world. Clearly, he was permanently influenced by his sense of isolation from the white majority and by his alienation from what he would invariably lambaste in his writings as the self-hating black bourgeoisie.

However, his college life was not altogether negative. At Howard he had what proved to be an invaluable exposure to black folk culture and black music—an exposure that would be as important to his writing as his readings in Western philosophy and Western literature. It was at this period, too, that he developed an interest in both the history of jazz and jazz criticism, an interest that would eventually lead to a career as one of the more significant jazz critics and historians of the 1960s.

After graduation from Howard University, Baraka satisfied the Selective Service requirements by enlisting in the air force. He spent some time serving in West Germany, but most of his tour was spent in Puerto Rico (1954–57). Baraka's air force experience seems to have intensified and broadened that sense of racial and cultural isolation which he first developed at Rutgers University. But here in Puerto Rico his feelings amounted to more than mere isolation. His was a growing and fundamental alienation from American society as a whole, from a sociopolitical system that he found culturally and racially incompatible, even repressive. As we shall see, this kind of alienation pervades the short stories which he wrote later with an air force setting.

The alienation had not yet taken specific directions, as far as a sense of alternatives was concerned. Instead we are left with impressions of an angry young air force sergeant—his rank upon discharge—who is a malcontent of sorts but who has yet to clarify his own options, beyond a certain rebelliousness. This rebelliousness was not overt in any significant way during the air force years. But it did lead to a marked withdrawal into his reading and into his writing. The reading extended the interests (Western philosophy and literature) that he had cultivated in college. And the writing included some of his earlier attempts at serious poetry.

On the whole his intellectual activities during this period typify a continuing ambiguity in Baraka's life as dissident or revolutionary: the intense and deepening alienation from America proceeds side by side with, indeed feeds upon, his active participation in American society: he is repelled by the air force and by the armed services generally as the quintessential symbols of the American system and the Western tradition as a whole, but his intellectual rebelliousness against these, and his early writings, are actually stimulated and influenced by his reading in America's literary and philosophical heritage.

After his discharge from the air force Baraka found himself in a position that was familiar to young blacks who had just completed their education or military service—or both. He had difficulty finding a job. And in his case the choices were sharply limited by his growing revulsion at the usual middle-class or working-class options—like the ones that had been chosen by his parents and his sister Sandra (a schoolteacher). He chose instead to settle down in Greenwich Village, in 1957, the year of his discharge from the air force. At this time the Village was the scene of the kind of intellectual and artistic ferment that lent itself readily to a genuine and substantive rebelliousness regarding the middle-class mainstream. The social atmosphere was decidedly liberal, racially integrated to a degree, and decidedly permissive. And it attracted considerable numbers of the politically alienated and the just plain disaffected, usually from affluent white families in the greater New York and surrounding areas.

On the whole, then, the Village was an ideal environment for a young black dissident whose racial alienation was not so militant as to be incompatible with a vigorous interest in the intellectual and artistic heritage of the white mainstream. The popular image of Baraka's earliest days in the Village is one of a newcomer joining an established circle of writers and other artists. But according to his first wife, Hettie Cohen, this was not actually the case.[2] Baraka met and married her within months after moving to Greenwich Village, and it appears that the circle of "beat generation" friends and associates actually developed after the marriage—largely as a result of the biracial couple's activities as writers and editors between 1958 and 1965.

They both worked for the *Record Changer Magazine*, where they actually met. They also founded and coedited *Yugen*, a literary magazine that they launched in 1958. During this period Baraka also worked as an editor at Totem Press, handling the works of such writers as Allen Ginsberg, Jack Kerouac, and Diane Wakoski. In 1961 he also joined forces with Diane Di Prima to launch and coedit yet another literary magazine *The Floating Bear*. And in that same year he founded with Di Prima the American Theater for Poets, an experimental writing and reading workshop. This was also the period when Baraka established himself as a young jazz critic of some substance, becoming a regular contributor to *Down Beat*, among other publications in the field.

Not surprisingly, these activities as writer, editor, and workshop organizer brought Baraka into contact with a large number of writers and other artists—the members of the so-called "beat generation" of intellectuals who made Greenwich Village their headquarters in the late 1950s and early 1960s. During these Village years his home became a center of sorts for informal activities and endless discussions. Regulars at these sessions included Di Prima, Ginsberg, Gregory Corso, and authors who were to be identified with the Black Mountain School of poetry—especially Charles Olson, whose ideas and practice were to have some impact on Baraka's own work, as we shall see in due course. This circle of friends and colleagues was predominantly white, but did include black jazz artists like Thelonius Monk and Ornette Coleman. And in this connection it should be noted that Baraka's work as writer and editor was complemented by his activities in the area of jazz: he was responsible for the organization of several workshops and concerts for the benefit of new, avant-garde jazz musicians.

The seven Greenwich Village years were also years of increasing prominence. The then LeRoi Jones was coming to the attention of the academic world and the so-called literary establishment. This was the period in which some of his earlier but major works were published— poetry: *Preface to a Twenty Volume Suicide Note* (1961) and *The Dead Lecturer* (1964); drama: *The Toilet* (1963), *Dutchman* and *The Slave* (1964); music criticism and history: *Blues People* (1963); and the novel, *The System of Dante's Hell* (1965). As his reputation as a radical young writer grew, so did the number of awards and other honors: a Whitney Fellowship (1960–61), the Obie Award, for *Dutchman* (1964), and the Yoruba Academy Fellowship (1965). Then there were the visiting lectureships, at the New School for Social Research (1962–65) and at the University of Buffalo (1964). In less than a decade the alienated young air force sergeant had become a young literary lion, basking in and profiting from his notoriety as all-round radical and black militant—at a time when the burgeoning civil rights movement was opening up a variety of opportunities to young black rebels.

Much of his writing in this period reflects the kind of radicalism that had been developing since the college years—an intense but vaguely defined rebelliousness that found its targets in racism, social injustice at home, and America's role abroad, especially in Third World countries. Three major events or experiences in the early 1960s stimulated this early radicalism and provided the impetus toward Baraka's subsequent development as social critic and writer-activist—the Cuban revolution, the emergence of Third World nations in Africa and elsewhere from the postwar remnants of European empires, and the racial violence of the 1960s in America itself.

In 1960 Baraka was among a group of black American writers who visited Cuba as the guests of Fidel Castro's fledgling revolutionary government. It is clear from one of Baraka's earliest collected essays ("Cuba Libre") that the visit had a profound effect on him. Castro's Cuba offered him a firsthand view of a revolutionary process in the making. And while it obviously did not make a Marxist revolutionary of him all at once, it jarred him into a new self-critical awareness about the limitations and contradictions in his own posture as radical and rebel within the fashionably dissident ambience of the "beat generation." Revolutionary Cuba offered Baraka his first concrete impressions of an alternative to the kind of system in which he had been participating with an increasing sense of separation. From here on his radical critique of America begins to acquire a sharper focus, despite the fact that the ideological substance of that critique has often been unimpressive.

The Cuban revolution also heightened his awareness of America's role abroad. What he saw as inadequacies at home were now complemented by the shortsightedness and moral bankruptcy with which America seemed to be responding to revolutionary and independence movements in the Third World. And on the whole this increasing radicalism merged with the growing militancy of the civil rights movement. The emergence of Black Power as a rallying cry in the middle 1960s signaled the degree to which a significant segment of the movement had shifted from civil rights protests as such to a militant emphasis on new political and cultural goals—specifically, greater political power for blacks, and a new emphasis on the distinctive qualities of black ethnicity and black history. These, at any rate, were the major rhetorical emphases of the black nationalist, or black cultural "revolution." These emphases coincided with the race riots that raced like brush fires through the major cities in the summers of the middle and late 1960s. And it is against this political background that the two crucial changes occurred in Baraka's personal life. In 1965 he separated from his wife, Hettie, from whom he was subsequently divorced. And in that year he moved from Greenwich Village to Harlem.

II   *The Emergence of Amiri Baraka*

A great deal has been said and written about the political implications of Baraka's marriage and divorce—particularly in light of the fact that his ex-wife is white. Interracial themes in his writings, especially in the earlier plays, have been viewed in relation to the author's relationship with his own wife; and conversely, there have been various attempts to link the break-up with Baraka's increasing black separatism. But much of this is mere speculation. Neither Baraka nor his former wife has really spoken in detail, at least for public consumption, about the cause-and-effect links between Baraka's political experiences and his domestic life. What is clear enough is that the changes in Baraka's personal life have been as inseparable from his political choices as those choices have been from his writings.

Hence his interracial marriage coincided with a period in his life when radicalism was not defined entirely in terms of black protest or black culture. The divorce took place at a time when he entered into his black separatist phase as black nationalist spokesman. And this black nationalist commitment coincided, in turn, with his marriage (1966) to a black woman, Sylvia Robinson. Finally, in the late 1960s he followed the prevailing trend among black nationalist spokesmen and their followers: he discarded the "slave names" that he had been given by his family. He chose a Muslim name that conformed with his concurrent conversion to the Muslim faith. Everett LeRoi Jones became Amiri Baraka (Blessed Prince).

From 1965 to 1970 Baraka's writings reflect the shift from civil rights protest to a belligerent black nationalism that celebrates the presumed distinctiveness of black culture and identity in America— his essays, *Home* (1966), his short stories, *Tales* (1967), his third major collection of poetry, *Black Magic* (1969), and the plays, *Baptism* and *Toilet* (1966) and *Four Black Revolutionary Plays* (1969). Much of the writing during this period centers on the stage, including not only these major works but also a substantial number of agit-prop pieces that were clearly intended as a species of political action—a means of mobilizing black community support for the ideals of the black nationalist program of local self-help and individual, ethnic pride. This kind of emphasis on the stage is a direct outgrowth of Baraka's increasing role as political activist during this period. And although the writings command attention in themselves, his reputation as black nationalist spokesman and activist clearly overshadowed his work as writer then—at least in terms of his general image.

After leaving Greenwich Village in 1965 he plunged into political activities on the local level. At first he briefly directed the Black Arts Repertory Theater, a community group in Harlem. The project was funded federally, through the Office of Economic Opportunity, but it soon foundered for lack of financial support when it came under attack for allegedly supporting works based on black racism and antiwhite violence. With the collapse of this project in 1965 Baraka returned to his old hometown, Newark, which has remained his headquarters and the focus of much of his political activism since then. As activist he concentrated on the major issue that was to dominate much of his writings from here on—the need for institutions and organizations (cultural and political) which could promote local self-sufficiency and mobilize broad political support for black nationalist causes.

To these ends he organized Spirit House, a community and arts center, shortly after returning to Newark. Two years later he founded Jihad Productions to support black nationalist artists; and in 1968 he joined the Committee for Unified Newark, and founded the Black Community Development and Defense Organization. These activities culminated on the local level in the 1970 elections when the groups with which he was associated worked successfully for the election of Newark's first black mayor, Bob Gibson. In fact, the 1970 elections became a standard example of what Baraka and others like himself now postulated as "Black Power"—the black community had been organized to use the existing political system and the electoral machinery to gain local political control in their own communities.

This phase of Baraka's political activism came to public attention in 1967 during the Newark riots when he was closely associated with one of the community groups, United Brothers of Newark. He was arrested on charges of unlawfully carrying firearms and of resisting arrest. His subsequent conviction was eventually reversed on appeal, and the case gained considerable notoriety—partly because of Baraka's own media image as a black militant leader, and partly because the conduct of the judge in the case sparked a spirited controversy, inside and outside legal circles, on his alleged intemperance and lack of judicial propriety in his handling of the defendant.

But this phase of Baraka's life as political activist and community organizer owes much more to a far less publicized but much more significant event. He taught as a visiting lecturer at San Francisco State College in the 1966–67 school year. And during that year he came under the influence of Ron Karenga, the West Coast black nationalist who had founded his own local group, US. Generally Karenga's "Kawaida" doctrine suffered from the same kind of intellectual thinness that plagued much black nationalist rhetoric in the 1960s and early 1970s. But Karenga did enjoy a certain appeal, largely because his vision of an effective black nationalism emphasized the need to supplement rhetoric with action, to make ethno-political ideals effective by building organizations and institutions for that purpose. His "Kawaida" principles, the ones that attracted Baraka very strongly, are essentially the formulation of pragmatic homilies on the need for social and political mobilization, with a continuing emphasis on those religious or deeply spiritual qualities which, allegedly, distinguish black history and culture worldwide.

Having spent much of his adult life in conscious rebellion against the prevailing systems of his society, Baraka was strongly attracted to Karenga's highly systematized approach to the definition of black power. In Karenga and his doctrines Baraka found ready-made means of articulating socioeconomic systems (local self-help) and political organizations (local community groups) which he translated with some limited success, to fit the needs of his political activities in Newark. Having also had a lifelong interest in world religions, he was naturally drawn to the religious emphasis of Karenga's brand of black nationalism.

Altogether the exposure to Karenga stimulated Baraka's interest in and enlarged his capacity for political organization. And this capacity led to his prominent role in the planning and holding of the 1970 Congress of African People in Atlanta. In retrospect the congress proved to be a watershed of sorts. It was largely a failure when considered as an attempt to weld the disparate elements of the black community into a single and influential political force. At best it succeeded in articulating an ideal—unity with diversity—which proved to be a statement of hope (or a thinly sugar-coated admission of irreconcilable differences) rather than any practical political platform. But notwithstanding its lack of any solid political achievement, the congress won national recognition for Baraka as an effective organizer and persuasive political leader: in the mass media, at any rate, he was the one who received much of the credit for whatever sense of unity and purpose did emerge from the congress.

After the congress Baraka's career as black nationalist is comparable with the black nationalist movement itself in the 1970s. Both went into swift decline. The black movement lost its impact as an explosive, potentially revolutionary force. America, specifically the white majority, was increasingly preoccupied with other crises, as the ubiquitous pollsters proved again and again—the war(s) in Southeast Asia, the economy, and more recently, energy crises; and that same majority has increasingly been convinced that racial relationships have improved, that things have changed for blacks, for the better, and—according to some whites—that blacks and other minorities have received too many concessions already as it is. The conservatism or apathy of the white majority regarding ethnic issues began to make itself felt at a time when several leaders of black militant groups, such as the Black Panthers and the Student Nonviolent Coordinating Committee, were arrested or fled into exile abroad. And, ironically, the more the white mainstream opened up opportunities to blacks, under pressure from militant black movements, the greater the loss of momentum for traditional and militant black groups alike: current and potential leaders of mass discontent became successful members of the mainstream.

This latter development was particularly irksome to Baraka, who eventually came to look with a jaundiced eye at the overall impact of integration. From his viewpoint that impact had had the effect of simply enriching the pockets and the political position of the black middle class. This is the viewpoint which he has articulated on frequent occasions in explaining his eventual shift from black nationalism to Marxist socialism (1974). Now America's racial and other social ills had to be tackled, not from an ethnic political perspective, but within the context of class divisions. The issue was no longer to be ethnic rebellion or cultural revolution defined in ethnic terms: it would be a class struggle to bring about the dictatorship of the proletariat.

The various changes in Baraka's political positions have tended to encourage a certain skepticism, even cynicism, about the man, especially about the depth of his ideological commitments. The actual ideological shifts have, of course, been obvious enough—the early apolitical rebellion of the beat generation, then the militant civil rights activism, followed in turn by black separatism and Marxist-Leninist socialism. The thinness or untidiness that has marked his adoption of these varying positions has also been obvious. But there is really no basis on which his sincerity or commitment to the ultimate issue can really be doubted. And that ultimate issue has remained consistent throughout all the twists and turns of his ideological choices: he remains steadfastly and deeply antipathetic to American mainstream culture—its social structure, its racial caste system, and its socioeconomic values. And the consistency with which he has remained a rebel against the mainstream has actually been highlighted, rather than diminished, by the very enthusiasm with which he continually seeks new approaches to change. Given his past record there is little reason to doubt that more ideological changes are possible, even likely. But it is also probable that he will continue to be motivated by the same deep-seated rebelliousness that has engaged him for much of his adult life—as activist and as writer.

CHAPTER 2

The Essays:
The Sense of the Prodigal

IN commenting on his first collection of published essays (*Home*) Baraka offers an observation that is applicable to his essays as a whole. The reader, he remarks, should get "the sense of the Prodigal" about the writer's life—a sense of movement and of "the struggle to understand where and who I am" (p. 9).[1] The essays do indeed provide a direct introduction to Baraka's rather varied career, one that begins on a fairly conventional note: a college education at Rutgers University and Howard University was followed by service in the United States Air Force. Thereafter, as a young writer, he joined the "beat generation" poets of Greenwich Village. Here his writings reflected that radical dissent from the American mainstream which he shared with comparable white writers, but which soon crystallized into a specifically racial rebellion against white America.

His move from the earlier radicalism of Greenwich Village to the Black Power politics of Harlem and Newark coincided with the political events of the middle 1960s when a new black militancy challenged the nonviolent tactics and integrationist goals of the older civil rights leadership. In fact although the shifts in Baraka's political attitudes have sometimes bemused admirers and detractors alike, the wandering of the prodigal has always followed a certain logic while being symbolic of social movements around him. It has been logical in that the political stance has always seemed to be the natural sequel to the previous position. Hence the black nationalism of the middle 1960s continues that revulsion at racial injustice and socioeconomic inequity which characterizes the earlier radicalism.

Similarly, Baraka's abandonment of black nationalism in favor of socialism actually confirms his lifelong radicalism. Moreover, although there has been no corresponding shift to socialism in black American politics at large, nonetheless Baraka's change is once again

27

symptomatic: it reflects a certain sense of anticlimax, even of disenchantment and failure, which seems to have replaced the populist energies of the Black Power movement in the 1960s. In this context, then, Baraka's switch to scientific socialism is not only a personal recognition of the failure of black nationalist politics. It also symptomizes a similar recognition in the society at large, one that is often implicit rather than explicit, but very real for all that.

All of Baraka's essays cover this period of growth and change, beginning with his 1960 essay on the fledgling Cuban revolution. The arrangement of the major collections reflects the patterns of change. Essays in *Home* trace his intellectual development from 1960 to 1965. *Raise Race Rays Raze* covers the evolution of his black nationalist ideology from 1965 to 1970. The essays written and published between 1970 and 1972 combine the continuing interest in black nationalist ideology with a more urgent preoccupation with the practical issues of political organization. And finally his 1975 essay confirms and explains his conversion to socialism. A similar evolution is detectable in the writings on black American art, especially on black music. *Blues People* (1963), the innovative history of the music, is comparable with the mood of the political essays of the same period: there is a delicate balance between an emerging separatist ideology and an impassioned protest that still accepts America as the black American's home. And the subsequent work, *Black Music*, is a collection of essays which reflect Baraka's gradual shift to an unequivocal black nationalism during the 1963–1966 period.

As an essayist Baraka's performance is decidedly uneven. The writings on music are always an exception. As historian, musicological analyst, or as a journalist covering a particular performance Baraka always commands attention because of his obvious knowledge of the subject and because of a style that is engaging and persuasive even when the sentiments are questionable and controversial. In this connection it is noteworthy that music is the only subject that Baraka consistently handles during his most militant black nationalist phase without abandoning an articulate persuasiveness in favor of mere abusiveness. Unfortunately this articulate style is not always, even at other times, in evidence in his other essays. The earlier pieces in *Home* are generally effective, uniting protest with incisive irony. The essay on the Cuban revolution combines journalistic descriptiveness with a certain degree of declamatory fervor, and as a result it is equally effective as information and as political judgment. But too many of the essays on politics and literature suffer from a stylistic thinness. This defect is often attributable to Baraka's increasing shift from a complex style of analysis and advocacy to the language of dogmatic statement and abuse.

There is also an intellectual thinness in many of the essays, irrespective of period. At his best Baraka is not an innovative thinker. His essays do not offer original insights into the nature of society; they do not really come to grips with the nature of revolution either as political process or intellectual experience; and they often gloss over the peculiar nuances and constructs of the artistic imagination in music or literature. In the absence of this kind of originality the engaging style of the early essays is an important asset, because it allows Baraka to restate a familiar position or idea with a clarity and a forcefulness that endow it with a convincing freshness. As he turns away from this kind of style, Baraka's essays are increasingly unconvincing.

But despite their limitations Baraka's essays are still of great importance to the student of his life and work. They demonstrate the significant phases of his intellectual growth. Consequently they illuminate both the major themes of his other writings and the links between those themes and Baraka's society. In examining the significance of these essays the present study divides them into two groups—political essays and essays on art (music and literature). To some extent this division is rather arbitrary and artificial since Baraka himself has always insisted in the essays on the intrinsic ties between art and politics. But this division is also convenient and useful: the political essays are therefore discussed first both because they introduce Baraka's political ideas per se and because they serve as introduction to his political perception of the arts in black America.

I *Political Essays: Protest and Rebellion*

"Cuba Libre," written after Baraka's visit to Cuba, is one of his frankest exercises in political self-criticism. The attacks on American society and on America's role abroad are counterbalanced by a candid appraisal of his own stance as radical protester. That stance is ambiguous. On the one hand there is a marked reluctance to deal with the everyday realities of a political event as far reaching as the Cuban revolution. His initial responses are based on a rather defensive determination to act as the poet whose role separates him from politics and therefore absolves him from having to take a stand on the issue of the revolution. Indeed, notwithstanding the atmosphere of radical politics in his Greenwich Village environment, it had never occurred to him until the Cuban visit that he could really attempt to find out what was actually happening in the world. And during the visit itself this cultivated image of the apolitical and uncommitted poet leads to friction with Cubans and other revolutionaries who despise the familiar notions of art-versus-society (*Home*, p. 42).

But on the other hand, he is interested in politics at this time, however much his response to a real (as opposed to a hypothetical) revolution might be inhibited by what some of his revolutionary critics saw as his cowardly bourgeois individualism. Although he vacillates between withdrawal and commitment there emerges from the essay as a whole the impression of significant growth from the role of detached writer-observer to that of impassioned ideologue. The ideology that emerges from the essay is, in effect, an evolutionary response to Cuba during the visit itself. And on this basis it fore-shadows the manner in which Baraka will consistently integrate new experiences with his radical predisposition.

He begins the visit, then, with the comfortable anti-middle-class snobbery of the young bourgeois radical—with the "proper knowing cynicism that is fashionable among my contemporaries" (*Home*, p. 20). It allows him to sneer at easy targets like black middle-class intellectuals visiting Cuba from Philadelphia, without having to ac-knowledge the limits of his own "radical" rebellion against the Amer-ican mainstream. But thereafter there is a discernible growth that is largely inspired by his direct confrontation with various aspects of the Cuban revolutionary reality—from the educational and agrarian re-forms to one of Fidel Castro's political rallies. The cynical "radical-ism" gradually gives way, by the end of the visit, to serious and disturbing questions, particularly questions about America's marked tendency to be on the reactionary side during fundamental upheavals in the Third World. And this new, more substantial rebelliousness is also more self-critical. He recognizes, for example, that incongru-ously enough in the politically conservative atmosphere of America the idea of rebellion and revolution is a recurrent and fashionable fad: "The rebels among us have become merely people like myself who grow beards and will not participate in politics" (*Home*, p. 61).

On the whole the "Cuba Libre" essay and the attitudes which it helped crystallize in Baraka himself clarify the kind of radical rebel-liousness which marks much of his earlier writing. He is repelled by socioeconomic inequities, by the middle-of-the-road blandness of the society as a whole, and by the "middle-brow" tastes that he attributes to most Americans. And the moral failures that he sees at home are duplicated abroad, in America's hostility to the Cuban revolution, for example. The growth of this rebelliousness after the Cuban visit is amply demonstrated by "The Dempsey-Liston Fight," an essay in which he sardonically treats the heavyweight fight as a recurrent allegory of some of America's least endearing qualities. The computer-staged "fight" between Dempsey and Liston is fraught with racial as well as broadly political overtones, and Baraka seizes upon them in what remains one of his best earlier essays. The work is itself written in the spirit of allegory, satirical allegory, as Baraka half-playfully surveys a series of heavyweight fights (real and computer-staged). The Liston-Patterson fights were contests between the Third World "primitive" (Liston) and neo-colonialism (Patterson, the black favorite of the white American boxing fan). Each time Patterson falls to Liston, then, Baraka has a vision of "the whole colonial West crumbling" (*Home*, p. 157).

In general Baraka's main target in these essays is the moral bankruptcy which he attributes to America's foreign and domestic policies, and the institutionalized hypocrisy which, in his view, sustains that bankruptcy. Hence America's role in the Third World is the more galling to Baraka because that role seems to contradict all of those values which Americans take for granted as their heritage—the idealization of America's "revolutionary" past, and the traditional rhetoric of freedom and equality. Baraka's revulsion at what he sees as America's institutionalized hypocrisies has two noteworthy consequences. In the long run it fuels his scorn for the contradictions between rhetorical idealism and political reality; and, conversely, it inspires a passionate quest, throughout his career, for a sense of sociopolitical unity and consistency, for a politically defined *wholeness* in which political contradictions and moral dichotomies are resolved. His angry fascination with institutionalized hypocrisy also explains, in part, the ideological restiveness which has marked much of his life. The young radical of "Cuba Libre," or the black nationalist and socialist of later years, is always frustrated by the enormous resources and deep-rooted strengths of a system which seems impervious to one form of attack or another.

In the short term Baraka's perception of double standards in America underlies his vigorous attack on white liberals in two of the essays published between "Cuba Libre" and "The Dempsey-Liston Fight"—"Letter to Jules Feiffer" (1961) and "Tokenism: 300 Years for Five Cents" (1962). It is erroneous to see these essays as unfair attacks

on well-meaning whites who actively promote the ideal of integration. But Baraka's attack in these works is rather selective and is
consequently more telling. For the real targets here are those attitudes which Baraka attributes to a traditional double standard in
America. First, there is that limited perception of black needs and
identity which allows whites to condemn racism while remaining
insensitive to the black need to define their racial identity in positive
rather than self-hating terms ("Letter to Jules Feiffer"). Second,
there is that ingrained hypocrisy (as Baraka sees it) which equates the
political gesture (limited or "token" integration, for example) with
substantive change ("Tokenism").

Moreover, social traditions like tokenism are not only symptoms of
the failure of American idealism. Tokenism also reflects another
major flaw. It represents a fallacious but popular notion of "progress." Progress is equated with political symbolism. The racial token
is therefore useful to the society because the appearance of the
"token" black in a symbolic act of integration enforces the cherished
idea that there has been meaningful and fundamental change—that
there has been "progress." The essay on tokenism therefore insists
that the only notion of substantive progress that has ever been
appealing or influential has been that of a quantitatively defined
progress based on the accumulation of wealth; and this limited definition of progress has too often substituted for a morally determined
commitment to the improvement of the human condition at all levels.

At this point it is easy to see how quickly Baraka has moved from
the awkward neutrality of his Cuban visit to an idealistic commitment
to radical social change. This commitment is both a reaction to the
shortcomings of America and a response to the Third World upheavals of the early 1960s. Thus in "Tokenism" Patrice Lumumba, the
slain premier of the Congo (Zaire), is the symbol of real change (that
is, revolutionary change) as opposed to token change. However, the
prorevolutionary sympathies which Baraka voices in an early essay
like "Tokenism" should not be confused with his later "scientific
socialism." These sympathies remain just that—sympathies rather
than a set of distinct ideological positions based on a clear enunciation
of alternatives to the existing system.

Nonetheless these prorevolutionary leanings are significant. In the
short term they are frequently the gestures of frustration, a rather
jejune espousal of Third World revolutions that compensates for a
sense of impotence in dealing with American society. But in the long
run Baraka's revolutionist gestures are obviously precursors of the

later, more ideologically defined, revolutionary phases (both black nationalist and socialist). And this attraction to the *idea* of revolution as fundamental change underscores that basic antipathy toward the status quo which informs all aspects of Baraka's political career.

The growing and deep-seated alienation that is inherent in Baraka's early prorevolutionism also brings into gradual focus the racial theme of his earlier essays. The "Cuba Libre" essay has ethnic implications. The visit to Cuba was possible because he and the other American invitees were black. But on the whole the racial issue is rarely more than incidental to Baraka's interest in Cuba itself. The issue becomes increasingly significant as Baraka is progressively alienated from American society. The "Letter to Jules Feiffer" and "Tokenism" essays are the first major pieces to deal with a predominantly racial subject. Both in "Tokenism" and "The Dempsey-Liston Fight" Baraka's general alienation from America is integrated with increasingly specific racial protest. Tokenism is therefore not simply a symptom of a limited and hypocritical concept of progress. It is also the effect of an intransigent racism.

In "The Dempsey-Liston Fight" the allegory of international politics is complemented by the drama of racial mythology. Liston is the "big bad nigger" of the white racial nightmare whose size and public image fulfill fearful fantasies about the black man's physical superiority. And having "demolished" the white Marciano and the (good) black Joe Louis alike in the computer-staged contests, he is defeated by that all-time superhero of boxing—Jack Dempsey, the Great White Hope par excellence. The age-old triumph of good over evil coincides with the reassertion of white superiority to black. Having imprisoned its psyche in one myth (the mental inferiority and physical superiority of blacks) white America tries to free itself by escaping, with the aid of the computer, into another myth (the physical and moral invincibility of its superheroes).

Baraka's exposé of racial myths is usually executed in a more direct and less engagingly ironic style than he employs in "The Dempsey-Liston Fight." The language of racial protest increasingly becomes more declamatory and abusive rather than analytical. The anger of the protester readily lends itself to the kind of facile racial invective which dominates the essays of the 1964–1966 period and which reflects the racial violence and urban riots of that time. Accordingly, "American Sexual Reference: Black Male" (1965) recalls the analysis of sexual phobias and racial myths in "The Dempsey-Liston Fight" two years earlier; but now the highly effective use of irony has given way to mere name-calling: "Most American white men are trained to be fags" (*Home*, p. 216). The acute intelligence which explores black-white sexual tensions seems curiously unable to reject those white racial clichés about the black stud, and now these clichés have been adopted to foster some notion of black sexual supremacy (*Home*, p. 233). At this point the protest against white racism takes on a self-indulgent emphasis, replacing one racial myth with another, and in the process drawing heavily on the culture's deep-rooted fears of homosexuality. On both counts, the racial and the sexual, the terms of Baraka's protest identify him more closely with the white American mainstream than he seems to recognize.

II *Political Essays: The Politics of Black Nationalism*

The emergence of blackness as a racial mystique in Baraka's earlier essays is partly due to his strategy of taunting white America with its own racial mythology and of goading white guilt with self-serving claims of inherent black superiority. But the essays in which these claims appear are not simply protest essays, if "protest" is understood here as a statement addressed to the offending "other" by the injured party. Essays like "American Sexual Reference" are simultaneously inward-looking and are aimed at the black community. In this respect the protest against white racism is interwoven with exhortations to black America on the superiority of black genes and on the need for black unity. The need for unity is emphasized in "What Does Non-violence Mean?" (1963) and "The Last Days of the American Empire" (1964). And in turn this emphasis on unity goes hand in hand with the increasing espousal of the cultural separateness of the black American.

This does not all happen overnight of course. The themes of black nationalism appear as early as 1962 in the antiintegrationist stance of "Tokenism" at a time when Baraka's writings are still dominated by the tactics of protest. Indeed there is really no contradiction between the protester and the nationalist at this time. His nationalism emerges in response to the gradual conviction that the goal of integration (which is always implicit or explicit in much of the protest movements) is unattainable and undesirable. The failure of protest therefore fuels his black nationalism. And as he is increasingly convinced of the essential futility of traditional protest, the rhetoric of protest becomes more strident, more designed to abuse than to convince. This explains the increasingly vituperative style which reaches its climax in the savage name-calling of "Newark Court-house—'66 Wreck" (*Raise*, pp. 3–9).[2] Conversely, the political definitions of black nationalism undergo a gradual evolution. At first there are a vague sense of global black unity and a deepening alienation from the white American mainstream; and then these are followed by outright separatism.

Two 1962 essays ("Black Is a Country" and "Street Protest") represent the early black nationalist mood. At this point Baraka's vision of a black nation is actually based on integrationist assumptions. Consequently "Black Is a Country" suffers from an intellectual fuzziness because Baraka is attempting to maintain two incompatible positions at the same time. On the one hand the essay seems to espouse the idea of a black American nation that is somehow comparable with the nations of Africa and Latin America. But on the other hand it is quite clear that Baraka is not thinking of black America as a *separate* nation. He contends that the idea of a black society within a white superstructure is useless, because blacks are Americans, but in the next breath declares, "The struggle is for independence, not separation—or assimilation for that matter" (*Home*, pp. 85–86). Baraka seems to sense the contradictions involved here and he attempts to resolve them by describing black American independence as "individual" independence or freedom. But the elaboration simply underscores the awkwardness and the superficiality with which the essay seeks to establish analogies between individualism and nationalism.

At this early stage the idea of black nationalism is badly undeveloped in Baraka's work, remaining little more than an evocative, catch-all phrase that reflects his vague sympathies with black liberation movements abroad. On the other hand the essays of the middle 1960s are less ambiguous and fuzzy. The call for political unity among blacks in "Blackhope" (1965) reflects the main thrust of the contemporary black power movement. He also advocates black nationalism as unequivocal separatism in "The Legacy of Malcolm X, and the Coming of the Black Nation" (1965). This latter essay represents three traits of Baraka's political writings. First, it exemplifies a disconcerting habit of adopting a new position, in this case black separatism, without once acknowledging his turnabout from a previous stance and without explaining the process that leads to the change. In the absence of such explanations, he frequently leaves himself open to charges of political opportunism. Second, it is quite obvious that his new nationalism is in direct response to the teachings of Malcolm X, and this influence typifies the degree to which much of his political writing serves the purpose of popularizing rather than originating political positions. Finally, this is the first major essay in which Baraka bases his arguments on some tangible philosophy—albeit Malcolm X's. Hence black separatism is described here as the logical outcome of the inherent incompatibilities between white and black cultures.

This basic cultural ideology is to remain an important aspect of Baraka's black nationalist writings even though it is not fully developed at the time of the Malcolm X essay. That development will not take place until the heyday of the black "cultural revolution" of the late 1960s. But until this ideological basis is fully developed his political stand as black nationalist is weakened by what at first appears to be merely an opportunistic switch to a popular mood.

III   *Black Nationalism and Black Culture*

Baraka does evince some interest in defining the distinctive nuances of black American culture before he actually commits himself to the idea of cultural separatism. But the earlier essays in which he demonstrates this interest are not particularly solid or helpful. "City of Harlem" (1962) offers the useless definition of the culture as "wild happiness" in the midst of "hatred and despair" (*Home*, pp. 92–93). And "Soul Food" (1962) is as limited in scope as its title suggests. But after 1965 the attempts to define black culture in substantive terms become more urgent as black nationalism becomes more central to Baraka's perception of America as a whole.

This urgency is best exemplified by the title and theme of "The Need for a Cultural Base to Civil Rites & Bpower Mooments" (1967). Baraka's "philosophy of blackness," as he calls it, claims spirit worship ("religious-science and scientific-religion") as the "special evolutional province" of black culture. This is the philosophy that has made the culture one of " peaceful humanists"; and since peaceful humanism has as its logical goal the "spiritual resolution" of the world, then it follows that a true black power movement must entail a cultural rebirth, or the reordering of the world (*Raise*, pp. 39–47). Moreover the spiritual humanism of black culture explains the alleged predisposition of blacks toward feeling in "Newark—Before Men Conquered" (1967). And since feeling is the key to human evolution, the future rests with blacks rather than with whites whose culture lacks feeling (*Raise*, pp. 59–81).

Baraka's philosophy of blackness is offered with the dogmatic preachiness that dominates the essays of this period and robs his arguments of persuasiveness. This is unfortunate because the tone often obscures a certain coherence or logical pattern in his ideas, even if those ideas may seem controversial or unfounded in fact. The emphasis on cultural evolution, for example, is not the conveniently contrived dogma of the moment that it might at first seem. It is actually a fairly logical outgrowth of Baraka's well-established reaction against that limited notion of progress which he attributes several years before to white American culture. Moreover, the evolutionary ideal in these essays complements very well the ideals of moral regeneration which Baraka's poetry had been exploring from as early as the prenationalist years of the early 1960s.

But curiously, although Baraka lays claim to the evolutionary ideal as the special province of blacks, it is not difficult to draw parallels between his emphasis on moral and cultural evolution and that ideal of progress which dominates American culture as a whole. For notwithstanding those superficial notions of progress which Baraka despises in the everyday reality of the mainstream culture, American idealism has always been motivated, at least in theory, by certain assumptions of human perfectability—from the "Founding Fathers'·'" lofty vision of a "more perfect union" to the political progressivism implied by a succession of presidential slogans ("new" deals, "new" frontiers, and "great" societies). Indeed, in attacking the superficialities of progress in the American reality Baraka is implicitly confirming that American idealism. And conversely, notwithstanding the exclusive blackness by which he defines his ideal of humanistic progress, Baraka's black nationalist criterion seems to stand squarely in the most optimistic traditions of American idealism. As we shall see in due course, this will not be the only occasion on which allegedly "black" criteria reflect affinities with the very American or Western values that black nationalists like Baraka are attempting to reject.

The emotional values that are inherent in Baraka's philosophy of blackness need more elaboration than he chooses to offer in "Newark—Before Men Conquered." In attacking the limits of white rationalistic culture the essay leaves the impression that antirationalism as such is some uniquely black value system. His general attitudes toward the subjects of reason and nonreason are not really different from those of other black writers, such as Malcolm X and the black theologian Joseph R. Washington, Jr. What these writers attack is not reason per se, but the abuse of reason in Western culture, where scientific rationalism seems to be prized at the expense of emotional values. Malcolm X is therefore able to admire the achievements of technological intelligence in Western culture while lamenting the inability of "the white man's working intelligence" to deal with human beings. And for his part Washington contrasts the prestige of the social *sciences* with their inability to solve problems (e.g., racism) created by human irrationality.[3] On the whole, then, writers like Malcolm X and Washington reflect a reasoned antirationalism rather than the embracing of irrationality as such. They are generally skeptical about the kind of scientific rationalism that has become a sacred cow in Western culture. And in a certain sense this is quite similar to an honorable and longlived tradition in Western culture itself: the eighteenth century caveats against single-minded rationalism are represented by works like Dryden's *Religio Laici* and Swift's *Gulliver's Travels*. And such works attest to the well-known fact that the emergence of modern science has always proceeded side by side with a philosophical skepticism that questions the notion of self-sufficient reason.

In light of all this, the real issue at stake in Baraka's espousal of spiritual values is not a simplistic dichotomy (black feeling versus white rationalism). Instead he questions the priorities of a culture in which the rationalistic mode is idealized at the expense of feeling, and in which the canons of scientific "truth" are often assumed to be incompatible with (therefore superior to) the "spiritual." And in the process he contrasts this dichotomy with the synthesis that he attributes to black culture, the synthesis of feeling and reason ("religious-science and scientific-religion").

This ideal synthesis therefore becomes the goal of that evolutionary movement which Baraka's black nationalism envisions. It represents an ethos of wholeness, one that is offered as a substitute for a rationalistic tradition in which insensitive systems (racial, socioeconomic, and philosophical) have fragmented communities and individuals alike. Consequently the wider consciousness that he envisages in "The Revolutionary Theatre" (1964) is the desired fulfillment of this ethos of wholeness. This is also the major theme of his novel, *The System of Dante's Hell*, where the young black protagonist develops from a self-destructive acceptance of white rationalism and puritanism to a more integrated self-consciousness based on the synthesis of intellect and feeling. Conversely, many of the poems of *The Dead Lecturer* are based on a recurring theme—the destructiveness of a narrowly technological culture that has too little room for passion and humanism.

The essays published between 1967 and 1972 expand on the ideal of wholeness. Three of the essays in *Raise Race Rays Raze* are pertinent here. "From: The Book of Life" (1967) is a rhapsody, celebrating blacks as beings of spirit whose religious heritage—especially by way of the African past—is integrated with their total experience instead of existing apart (*Raise*, pp. 49–55). And by virtue of this heritage black culture comes closer to that ideal of wholeness which Baraka celebrates in another essay, "Meanings of Nationalism" (1969): "Science and religion must be absolutely identical" (*Raise*, p. 107).

In "Mwalimu Texts" (1970) the philosophical ideal of "one-ness" or wholeness has an immediate and practical application in the political strategy of operational unity—that is, ethnic unity among blacks, the unification of political movements within the black community, and a general emphasis on effective political organization. In fact the very idea of organization is both a practical political necessity and the microcosm of a larger evolutionary movement in which "progress," as defined by Baraka's "black" humanism, connotes a movement toward perfection. And this movement should culminate in ethnic, global, and cosmic experiences of wholeness: "We are after the perfection of our species and the evolution of men and their motives to the furthest reaches of life. All life joined in symbiotic understanding" (*Raise*, p. 166).

The concept of operational unity, like so many of his other criteria, is borrowed from elsewhere. It is derived from Ron Maulana Karenga, the leader of US (as opposed to "them"), a militant black nationalist group. The idea of operational unity appeals to Baraka not simply because it is the political version of a philosophical ideal, but also because by invoking that ideal in the political arena he is integrating political *activism* with idealistic *vision*. And in this process, of course, he is literally attempting to demonstrate the fundamental ideal itself. This is the kind of demonstration that he undertakes in those essays which are really guidelines or manuals on political strategy. These include the introductory essay to *African Congress: A Documentary of the First Modern Pan African Congress* (1972), where he acknowledges Karenga's influence, and an article in *Black World* (October 1972), "Toward the Creation of Political Institutions for All African Peoples."

However, the most extended demonstration of operational unity is the major publication of the later years of Baraka's black nationalism, *Kawaida Studies: The New Nationalism* (1972). The book is really a frank attempt to popularize Karenga's brand of nationalism, the "new" nationalism that differs from the old (middle 1960s) because the former is more concerned with the ideals of black nationalism as a cultural tradition and with the mundane details of political organization. Consequently the major principles of Karenga's group as they are expounded by Baraka quite adequately summarize the basic elements of operational unity in political and philosophical terms: umoja (unity), kujichaagalia (self-determination), ujima (collectivism), ujamaa (cooperative economics), kuumba (creativity), and imani (faith) (pp. 9–10).[4]

On the whole Baraka brings together his criteria for unity and wholeness rather well. His success is partly due to the manner in which the concept of unity is shown to be a natural reaction to those fragmenting forces which he attributes to Western culture. It is also due to the thoroughness with which these later essays on black nationalism apply his basic ideal of wholeness to a variety of subjects (religion, political organization, economics, or personal growth and social change in general). In so doing these essays represent a fully integrated argument, and actually become, in the process, a rhetorical demonstration of the kind of philosophical and moral synthesis that they describe. The total effect is one of an impressive coherence in the overall presentation of his philosophy, the more impressive because the style and achievement of any single essay still suffer from a dogmatic and generally shrill tone. But despite these limitations, every essay serves Baraka's purpose precisely because the uninhibited expression of feeling (i.e., dogmatic fervor) supplements his basic thesis—the importance of feeling and spiritual energy.

But however impressive these essays may be in terms of their composite rhetorical effect, they are not altogether convincing as definitions of black cultural nationalism. Even at their strongest point, the consistency with which they apply Baraka's ideal of wholeness to the black experience, the essays reflect a certain sloppiness that gives rise to obvious contradictions. Throughout *Kawaida Studies*, for example, Baraka envisages the brave new world of blackness in strictly urban terms. Newark, New Jersey, where Baraka himself was an active political organizer of the late 1960s, is repeatedly offered as the model of the new black nation—culturally separate, socioeconomically self-sufficient, and politically independent of white America. It is never clear how rural black America—which does exist—will fit into this black urban millennium; and Baraka, a northern black with no direct personal ties to the rural South, never bothers to ask or answer the question.

Moreover, in view of the urban bias of his cultural and political perception, the "African" criteria of his ideology are rather suspect. For in offering the philosophical arguments of Karenga as African-derived modes, it never seems to occur to Baraka (any more than it apparently did to his mentor Karenga) that urban culture, as he envisages it on behalf of the black nation, is closer to the high-density, compacted life-style of Western urban culture than it is to the African models (especially Julius Nyerere's Tanzania) from which he culls the cultural criteria of *Kawaida Studies*. In the final analysis we are left with black nationalist criteria which (once again) are closer to Western culture than their advocates seem willing or able to admit.

On the whole, contradictions of this sort leave the impression that the "African" criteria of black American nationalism are at best a well-intentioned but essentially sentimental incongruity. At worst even the good intentions lend themselves to a certain kind of manipulativeness, as they do in the notorious case of the "Kwanzaa" festival which Karenga invented for black Americans while claiming that it was a genuine African tradition.[5] The ersatz nature of such ideas, together with the contradictions inherent in others, limits the usefulness of the black philosophical idealism that Baraka espouses, notwithstanding the impressively integrated design of his rhetorical methods. In short, his black nationalist rhetoric enjoys a coherence of sorts but it lacks depth. There is no adequate body of data to support the philosophical claims and the political objectives. For example, there is no demonstration that black Americans have really managed to preserve some African-derived communality in the aggressively individualistic context of American society. And in the absence of such proof we are left with merely a prescriptive preachiness: these things must be so, and if they are not then the fault lies somewhere in the self-hating, "white" standards of the integrationist black middle class.

Given the intellectual shortcomings of Baraka's black nationalism it is not surprising that his concept of "blackness" often suffers from the kind of ideological thinness about which Harold Cruse complains when he surveys in *The Crisis of the Negro Intellectual* (1967) the attempts of black Americans to formulate social ideologies of any kind, integrationist or nationalist. In lieu of intellectual substance

Baraka's philosophy of blackness is often little more than racial invective, aimed at whites in essays like the 1968 work "Article/Story About Newark Policeman Using Their Real Names" (*Raise*, pp. 91–96). Baraka occasionally feels compelled, as he does in "Meanings of Nationalism" (1969), to explain that this invective is not racist as such, but is a response to the hatefulness of white racism—a "legitimate empirical reaction" (*Raise*, pp. 105–106). But the racial name-calling ("wops", "white boys," and so forth) is self-defeating. The line between the black victim's sense of moral superiority and the black nationalist's claims to racial superiority is never clearly drawn. And the antiwhite invectives too often function as a transparent substitution for solid definitions of a distinctive blackness—assuming that such definitions are available in any form except as dogmatic generalizations.

These generalizations sometimes take the form of shallow posturing. "What Does Nonviolence Mean?" (1963) claims that blacks are the only "revolutionary" force in America (*Home*, p. 151). But the claim does violence to the meaning of "revolutionary" while ignoring the complex nature of black American protests which have often seemed geared, even in their most violent forms, to force integration within the existing social structure rather than to restructure (i.e., revolutionize) the society. By a similar token, Baraka is unconvincing when "City of Harlem" claims that black America is a community of nonconformists, on the ground that the mere fact of being black places blacks in the situation of being "weird" (*Home*, p. 93). He seems unaware that conformity, or nonconformity, is not simply a matter of situation per se but of responses to that situation, and that like many excluded or disadvantaged groups black Americans have been known to be conformist (integrationist) precisely because the outsider's circumstances encourage a certain need to belong. And on those occasions when he does take note that some black Americans do conform Baraka's easy solution is to exclude them from the sphere of a proper blackness by dismissing them as middle-class "Negroes" throughout the essays.

Baraka is also unconvincing when he does offer specific plans for the realization of the black nationalist millennium. For example, "The Practice of the New Nationalism" (1970) envisages the black takeover of American cities, complete with total political control and the nationalization of economic institutions within the cities. But he does not indicate how this could ever be effected in the face of the enormous power which already controls the cities. And at this juncture Baraka's black nationalism seems to be little more than a strident wish-fulfillment (*Raise*, pp. 159–64). It amounts to a rhetorical device that is often more useful in enumerating and lambasting the evils of white racism than in defining black American culture as a distinctive entity.

IV *Scientific Socialism*

Baraka's shortcomings as a black nationalist thinker are symptomatic of the intellectual anemia which has limited the potential of black cultural nationalism as a political force. In turn the decline of the "cultural revolution" of the middle 1960s clearly disillusioned Baraka, and as he himself eventually acknowledges black nationalists like himself erred in defining black American culture simply as an extension of Africa. This acknowledgment is offered in the pivotal *Black World* essay "Why I Changed My Ideology," in which Baraka uncharacteristically takes pains to explain his switch from one position to another—in this case the move from black nationalism to socialism.[6] On the whole, quite apart from its own merits, Baraka's scientific socialism is particularly useful to the student of black nationalism and of Baraka's contributions to black nationalism, because as a socialist writer Baraka is obviously candid about the limitations of the ethnic movement.

In addition to conceding the intellectual limitations of black nationalism Baraka also pinpoints a paradoxical aspect of the movement: despite its avowedly separatist, antiestablishment rhetoric, the movement's real accomplishment was to create a political atmosphere of tension and confrontation which pressured white society into making concessions; but these concessions actually encouraged integration rather than separation by opening up opportunities to blacks, to those whom Baraka attacks as the "black petite bourgeoisie" who had "grown fat off the gains made by the struggle of the people."

Quite apart from the reasons that he offers for the failure of black nationalism, Baraka's switch to socialism actually completes a cycle of sorts in his intellectual development. Hence his admission that the black nationalist was unrealistic in treating black Americans as Africans returns him to an earlier position that has already been noted in his essays—that however distinctive, the black American experience is basically American. Similarly, this socialist phase seems, in retrospect, to be a culmination of the curiosity and the sympathies that were first stirred by the early visit to Cuba. For despite the black nationalist interlude both the early interest in Third World revolution and the more recent commitment to socialism are the outgrowth of a certain commitment to the ideal possibilities of American society, a commitment that accentuates his revulsion at the failures of the society, without (apart from his black nationalist phase) inspiring the need to reject it in its entirety. In abandoning racially defined approaches to the problems of American society, Baraka is therefore reaffirming some of his earliest perceptions of his society. In this light his conversion to socialism is less capricious than it at first seems and actually reflects a long-range consistency in his political views.

However, this underlying consistency does not really compensate for the unsatisfactory features of Baraka's socialist arguments. Although he acknowledges those shortcomings which limited the usefulness of black nationalism, he is less than candid about his personal contradictions in moving from ethnic to socialist criteria. For example, he is now quite contemptuous of those black nationalists who are suspicious of socialism on the ground that it is a "white" ideology. Scientific truth, Baraka admonishes, is "universally applicable." The admonition would have been more impressive had Baraka also taken the pains to admit that he himself previously rejected socialism as a "white" ideology in black nationalist essays like "Article/Story About Newark Policemen Using Their Real Names" (*Raise*, pp. 95–96).

This lack of self-criticism is awkward, suggesting as it does a certain lack of candor about the contradictions and reversals that are inherent in his intellectual development. It is also disconcerting because it reinforces the impression that Baraka has simply drifted from one set of ideas to another without having seriously thought about their implications in their own terms and in light of his political growth. The underlying antipathies to the American mainstream have remained consistent, but the manner in which Baraka offers his ideological changes unduly encourages the impression of both opportunism and superficiality. Even at this point Baraka has yet to learn how to deal in a persuasive way with ideas or how to describe convincingly his changing relationship with ideas.

This continuing failure amounts to one of the less desirable consistencies in Baraka's political essays: in moving from one ideology to another he seems to lack intellectual substance. No feature of the *Black World* essay on socialism exemplifies this more painfully than the language. Baraka's emphasis on the scientific dimensions of his latest ideology stands in incongruous contrast with a style which is little more than a series of clichés strung together to produce a harangue. It is a far cry from the imaginative ironies of earlier essays like "The Dempsey-Liston Fight," and the heavy reliance on the use of shrill clichés has the effect of tired bombast rather than persuasively scientific logic:

> Build revolutionary fronts!
> Expose the illusion of bourgeois democracy and rip the covers off
>   their lackeys!
> Let the people find out armed struggle is inevitable!
> Victory to Black people!
> Victory to the strugglers!
> Victory to all oppressed people!

This kind of language is functional only in a rather perverse way: the hackneyed phrasing complements perfectly the superficial level on which Baraka attempts to explain his ideology. Instead of scientific analysis he merely recites secondhand slogans, and at this point there is little to distinguish his political essay from the political poster.

V   Baraka's Style as Political Essayist

The problems posed by the language of this *Black World* paper are also linked with Baraka's relationship with the role and nature of language itself, both as political statement and as a form of political activism. This relationship shifts with his ideological growth. In the early essays of the *Home* collection where he thinks of himself as observer ("Cuba Libre") he favors a dispassionate and analytical style which serves an ironic function precisely because it contrasts with his gradual rejection of a "dispassionate" political stance. This kind of ironic detachment is best exemplified by the language of "The Dempsey-Liston Fight," but as his political commitment intensifies, especially in ethnic terms, his political fervor seems to leave little room for analytical discourse—even of the intensely ironic kind. In the black nationalist phase declamation and invective are the main methods. Hence passionate exhortation rather than persuasion seems to be the real purpose of a work like "The Last Days of American Empire" (1964), which is included in the *Home* collection: "Death throes of the empire. UGLY CRACKERS! Negro policemen with sad twisted eyes. Strong faces. . . . ALL KINDS OF VICTIMS.

People being burned. What does America mean to you?" (*Home*, p. 189).

At the same time, however, the rhetorical excesses of the black nationalist essays also reflect a certain restiveness on Baraka's part with the effectiveness of language itself, especially the written word, as the tool of political activism. The shift from an earlier reliance on analytical modes therefore suggests the conviction that such a method is of limited usefulness to his increasingly activist bent. Now the concern is with reaching an audience, particularly an audience of the converted, or of those predisposed toward conversion. And in such circumstances the language of the essayist is primarily meant to move his audience toward action. The "black English" of "Raise! Raise!" (1968) is an example of this pragmatic consideration. It is based on the practical need to identify and address an ethnically "appropriate" audience: "Somebody tawkin always bees tawkin to each other. We meets and stands around and dbaits" (*Raise*, p. 83).

The reference to debate here is double-edged, connoting both the usefulness of debate and the pitfalls of substituting talk for action. This uneasiness with "talk" as debate or analysis explains Baraka's approach to the essay as political statement. He is increasingly more interested in the form as a mode of activism, as a thinly disguised manual for political action, rather than as a forum of debate and explication for their own sake. This is particularly true of the *Kawaida Studies* collection. Hence "Strategy and Tactics of a Panafrikan Nationalist Party" is little more than a set of directives on such practical issues as the appointment of cadres and the building of political platforms. And in this essay Baraka is quite explicit about his reservations toward political language as opposed to political action: "We must not be so drunk with the rhetoric of revolution that we do not actually go about the business of making immediate change. Words are not immediate change. . . . The most revolutionary Afrikans . . .will be those who can deliver those goods and services. Who can actually take visible power" (p. 51).

In the long run, then, the unevenness of Baraka's essay style since the late 1960s stems not only from the thinness of his ideological positions but also from his clear movement away from analytical and descriptive forms to half-developed forms which seem intended to exploit language not simply as talk but as action, political action. The analytical modes which he inherits in the essay as genre conflict with needs that become more urgent as his political activism is intensified.

As we shall see in due course Baraka also strains against the inherited forms of the other genres in which he writes; and in his best poetry or prose fiction he succeeds in creating innovative forms in the very process of assaulting traditional forms and styles. This kind of success eludes him in most of his later political essays: having abandoned the traditional analytical techniques and having attacked the very idea of an effectively activist political language, he fails in due course to develop an effective substitute, and he is left instead with the dreadfully formulaic clichés of his *Black World* paper on socialism or with the dogmatic repetitiveness of most of the black nationalist essays.

This all has important implications for Baraka's perception of writing in general. The exhortations, the set formulae of political dogma, the alternation between standard and nonstandard English (especially in the black nationalist papers)—all these features of the later essays reflect an interest in the essay form not as a vehicle for analytical and descriptive statement, but as a kind of art form, one that approximates the art of the pulpit. And this interest in the artistic possibilities of the essay makes it only appropriate that Baraka's essays also include works on the nature and function of art.

VI *Essays on Black American Art*

There are significant links between Baraka's political essays and his essays on black American music and literature, and these parallels emphasize the intrinsic links between politics and art in his work as a whole. First, his complaints about the political shortsightedness of white liberals are comparable with his attack on white jazz critics. In "Jazz and the White Critic" (1963), for example, the culprits are white critics who are ignorant of or are hostile to the distinctive qualities of black American music.[7] Second, that ideal of wholeness which informs so much of his political philosophy, especially in the black nationalist period, is also fundamental to his literary and music criticism; and it accounts for his repeated insistence on a view of art which integrates aesthetics and ethics (beauty and moral function), form and content. Third, as in his political essays Baraka's criteria as critic begin with the perception of black American culture and art as inseparably American phenomena; but these criteria eventually give way to a separatist view of the arts in black America, to the "black aesthetic" criteria of the "Black Arts Movement" of the late 1960s and early 1970s.

VII *Baraka and the Black Aesthetic*

The black aesthetic views of Baraka's later essays are the culmination of his work as a critic. But they are also partially implicit in some of the earlier works on music and literature. Moreover, by virtue of his writing and his work as political organizer for community arts centers, Baraka emerged as one of the leaders of the Black Arts Movement in the 1960s. And given his long involvement with the black aesthetic issue it is necessary to review the arguments raised by the issue during the past sixteen years. These arguments have often been obscured by the acrimonious nature of the debates that center on the black aesthetic and by the imprecise language of the black aesthetic proponents themselves. However, on the whole, claims on behalf of a black aesthetic seem to fall into two broad categories.

First there are the statements of protest which decry the ignorance or bias with which outsiders (that is, white critics) approach black American art. Then there are the theories which claim that black art arises from a uniquely black cultural tradition and that it therefore requires a critical approach rooted in the special experiences of black culture.[8] On the whole the proponents of the black aesthetic have been most persuasive when they attack the shortcomings of established literary criticism in relation to black literature, for example. For in so doing they demonstrate the degree to which racial bias and outright ignorance of the black writer's experience have fostered a limited, and often distorted, criticism. In other words, on this level the black aesthetic argument is doing little more than insisting upon that sound knowledge of subject and subject area which ought to be the prerequisite in the study of any body of literature.

At the same time the supporters question the scholarly critic's traditional tendency to insist on the universality of art. They see this insistence as a kind of evasion because, in their view, the critic's insistence that "serious" art transcends racial, regional, and cultural considerations simply allows the critic an erudite rationale for shirking the responsibility of learning about those considerations in the first place. The "universal" criterion is particularly susceptible to this kind of attack, but not because black aesthetic supporters necessarily deny that black art can have a "universal" appeal. The criterion is suspect in this context because its application to nonwhite literature often smacks of a racial double standard. Hence the history of Western literary criticism is replete with sociopolitical, religious, regional, and philosophical approaches to Western writers (Shakespeare, Milton, Dostoevski, and Tolstoy, for example); but there has been a tendency to dismiss the social and ethnic themes of black literature as incompatible with serious art since the latter is supposed to transcend mere race and ethnicity.[9]

Altogether, then, the arguments on behalf of the black aesthetic are most effective as protests against the failures of established criticism. But the related attempts to define the black aesthetic as an aesthetic per se have been less successful. Despite the frequent pronouncements on the subject, no one has yet demonstrated convincingly that a black aesthetic actually exists as a uniquely "black" mode of creating and perceiving art. The differences between the social and racial experiences of black and white Americans, for example, may be adequate grounds for demanding, as we have already seen, that nonblack critics acquire some knowledge of the social milieu of the black artist. But although cultural differences create the need for this kind of critical practice, it does not necessarily follow that they also result in a wholly distinctive aesthetic. The South African writer, Ezekiel Mphahlele, for one, is not persuaded that such an aesthetic exists: "Clearly, what is referred to as a black aesthetic has emerged as a *black point of view so far.*" [10]

The kind of black aesthetic criteria that arouses Mphahlele's skepticism here is usually offered as an antithesis to a "white" aesthetic. Addison Gayle, Jr., one of the more articulate proponents of this view, perceives the "white" aesthetic as a single-minded approach to art "for art's sake," with no interest in the expressive functions of art. And on the other hand the "black" aesthetic is defined as a functional view of art, one which rejects the ideal of "art for art's sake." But at this point the black aesthetic merely reflects a politically self-serving but historically inaccurate view of Western criticism. Western aesthetics have always been a welter of diverse, frequently conflicting schools. The esoteric position has always flourished in Western aesthetics; but then so has the functional view, and the latter (represented by the Fabians and the Marxist-Leninists, for example) does not seem to be intrinsically different from what is now being offered as a unique black mode.

The suspect intellectual basis of the black aesthetic is further weakened by a tendency to offer these unproven aesthetic claims as prescriptive norms for critic and artist alike. The dubious claim that the black aesthetic represents a unique black ethos has been compounded by the demand that black artist and black critic must observe that criterion. Thus, according to Gayle, the critic's judgment should not be based on considerations about the beauty of the work itself. The critic should be concerned instead with determining whether the work has transformed "an American Negro into an African-American or black man." [11] But this prescriptiveness makes no allowance for a variety of approaches to black American arts, approaches that may include (without being limited to) critical perspectives and artistic forms which do not fit comfortably into political definitions of a proper "blackness."

The limitations of the black aesthetic school have also been compounded by a certain intellectual thinness, one that has resulted in a marked failure to define precisely the very nature of the aesthetic experience itself. Very few attempts have been made, throughout this debate, to come to grips with the *idea* of an aesthetic. The usual practice has been to toss out the term "aesthetic" as a vaguely evocative catch-all that haphazardly covers a medley of subjects ranging from art and food to politics and morality. And this medley has often been more useful as political rhetoric than as the study of the relationship between black culture, black art, black critics—and black politics. The repetitive arguments of the black aesthetic usually gloss over the primary notion of aesthetics as modes that describe the form and nature of art and the critical responses to art. And as a result there has yet to be a convincing theory of the "black aesthetic" as a process that deals not simply with political issues for their own sake, but with the special ways in which artist or critic responds to the peculiar properties of a work of art *and* to the relationship between that art and its cultural sources. In view of this failure the black aesthetician has yet to prove that a black aesthetic actually exists.

Among the major proponents of the black aesthetic only Baraka has made any significant attempt to deal with the idea of an aesthetic as such. Thus he asks what "aesthetic" means in his essay "The Fire Must Be Permitted to Burn Full Up" (1970). Subtitled "Black Aesthetic," the essay is a deliberate attempt to redefine "aesthetic," to dissociate the term from an assumed "white" value system and to infuse it with connotations that are, presumably, distinctly black: ". . . shdn't it mean for us Feelings about reality! The degrees of in to self registration. Interest. About Reality. In to selves. Many levels of feeling comprehension. About Reality. . . . Not a theory in the ether. But feelings are central genuine & descriptive. . . . So a way of feeling (or the description of the process of) is what an aesthetic wd be" (*Raise*, p. 117).

In so far as he consciously attempts to define his terms Baraka

avoids some of the fuzziness that results from using the term "aesthetic" without regard for its traditional connotations. At least he
appears to recognize that he needs to redefine the term for the sake of
clarity before proceeding to apply it to his "black" aesthetic criteria.
This does not mean, of course, that his criteria are necessarily convincing on their own terms. In advocating feeling as the definitive
value of black art he is offering the usual antithesis between an
exclusively ethereal, nonfeeling response to art in Western culture
and black art as black feeling. As usual this kind of contrast is both
distortive and prescriptive—distortive in that it ignores the diverse
approaches to the nature of art in Western culture, and prescriptive
in that it is now offered as the sole imperative for black nation-
building through the arts (*Raise*, p. 121). But although Baraka has
come to be associated almost exclusively with the black aesthetic
approach to black American art, it is a position that developed only
gradually in his writing. And the course of that development reveals
his strengths as well as his weaknesses as a critic of black music and
literature.

VIII   *Black Music and Black American History*

Much of Baraka's early criticism is in the field of jazz and has been
reprinted in his *Black Music* collection (1967). These essays include
materials that originally appeared as "liner notes" for jazz recordings
and represent Baraka's significant strength as a critic. He combines
an incisively analytical style with a penchant for the thought-
provoking generalization, the kind of generalization that is usually
rooted in an obvious wealth of knowledge however outlandish it
might at first seem. In this vein "The Jazz Avant-Garde" (1961) is not
only an entertaining, precisely written analysis of bebop as a new
development in jazz, but it is also a definition of jazz as a uniquely
American art form. For Baraka the evolution of this art form involves
the constant incorporating of new modes within existing traditions
and styles. And this process represents a notion of avant-garde that he
distinguishes, as a broad philosophy, from a narrower perception of
the avant-garde. The narrow view is *disjunctive* in that it distinguishes between past and present in more exclusive, separatist terms
than does Baraka's *conjunctive* perception of the traditional and the
new: "I am trying to explain 'avant-garde.' Men for whom history
exists to be *utilized* in their lives, their art, to make something for
themselves and not as an overpowering reminder that people and

their ideas did live before us" (*Black Music*, p. 71). This insistence on the wholeness of history and experience (that is, the integration of past and present) anticipates that sense of wholeness which is to dominate his later views of art and society.

Similarly the emphasis on jazz as an American form foreshadows that later black nationalist phase. The emphasis is a form of cultural nationalism in a broad American sense, in that it is offered by way of attacking America's cultural colonialism. In his view the American's colonial mentality is reflected in the national tendency to assume that only European "art" (i.e., classical) music is "serious" music. In turn this American cultural nationalism that Baraka espouses here anticipates the later black nationalism in that Baraka obviously attributes the uniquely American aspects of jazz to the roots of black American musical forms like bebop. It is important to emphasize this link between Baraka's indelible American consciousness and his black nationalist aesthetics precisely because as a black nationalist he so often and vigorously repudiates the possibilities of such a connection. For despite his separatist protests to the contrary it appears that much of black American nationalism is dominated by a broadly American rather than uniquely "black" ethos, that whether a Baraka espouses an ideal of genuine (black) progress rather than a specious (white) revolutionism, or whether he defines black America's cultural heritage in "anti-colonial" (i.e., antiwhite) terms, he is drawing upon an American tradition of philosophical idealism which fosters the *idea* of progress and which is, theoretically, at least, opposed to colonialism (apropos of Europe's cultural and political hegemony in the New World).

In the early 1960s Baraka did not necessarily repudiate the fundamentally American basis of his critical approaches to music. Hence his major study of black American music, *Blues People* (1963), stresses the American character of black music in much the same way that his earlier political essays define black culture as part of rather than separate from the American mosaic. The development of black music is therefore conceived as the blacks' "transmutation from African to American." [12] This recognition of black American music as the product of a total American experience also accounts for the painstaking care with which *Blues People* traces the development of black musical forms as the synthesis of different traditions, including the African.

The study is pervaded by a sense of cultural synthesis, one that clearly arises from Baraka's fundamental view of history. As in that earlier essay on the avant-garde, *Blues People* reflects a historical perspective that enhances a sense of the coexistence of past, present, and future while encouraging a view of American history as one which interweaves a variety of cultures without obliterating any single one. This kind of perspective clearly anticipates his black nationalist sense of wholeness. And since this incipient sense of ideal wholeness does not allow for the arbitrary separation of art (in this case, music) from social experience, then the study's prevailing theme (black American music *as* black American history) is a recognizable precursor to his later insistence, as black nationalist, on the integration of form and content, aesthetic design and feeling.

It is important to emphasize the social and historical orientation of *Blues People* because even a perceptive reader like Ralph Ellison has taken Baraka to task for failing to achieve something that the study deliberately avoids—namely the description of black music as a form that transcends the conditions of the black community itself.[13] *Blues People* avoids a "transcendental" view of black music precisely because Baraka simply declines to perceive art as something that transcends its historical and cultural sources into some region where art is "pure" art. Neither is this choice due to some disregard on Baraka's part for the distinctive nuances which differentiate art from *other* reflections of historical and cultural processes. Hence in the same year in which *Blues People* was published the compelling and lovingly crafted essay on Thelonius Monk ("Recent Monk") demonstrates Baraka's ability to describe an art form (in this case Monk's performance) by highlighting not only the artist's social environment but also the distinctive features of his art form, as art (*Black Music*, pp. 26–34).

IX *Black Music and the Black Aesthetic*

On the whole, then, *Blues People* is a significant event in Baraka's intellectual development because it so clearly enunciates a view of history and art that is to be increasingly crucial to Baraka's politics and aesthetics: art forms, like history itself, evolve as organic modes that exemplify the writer's perception of experience as an inviolable whole; and in turn that sense of cosmic wholeness is reinforced by the integration of history and art.[14] This sense of integration is also pertinent to Baraka's developing interest in a black aesthetic. It implies the functional context which the black aesthetic claims as its special province. And in discussing specific musical traditions Baraka is quite explicit in attributing functional roles (particularly protest roles) to such forms as work songs and the blues.

It is in the later essays of *Black Music*, however, that Baraka's music criticism most clearly reflects the black aesthetic as an ideology. In this sense "Jazz and the White Critic" typically castigates the racial biases and cultural ignorance of white music critics (*Black Music*, p. 14). But on another level the aesthetics of Baraka's music criticism is also claiming a peculiar "black" dimension in musical art. Hence in 1966 he offers a black (music) aesthetic in "The Changing Same (R & B and New Black Music)": history and (African-derived) religious practice have produced a particularly spiritual dimension in black American culture, a culture of feeling in which the aesthetics of music must be defined in terms of emotion and spirit (*Black Music*, p. 182). Expressed in separatist terms, this view of black music as black spirit complements the emphasis on the perceived differences between white and black arts: "We want different contents and different forms because we have different feelings. We are different peoples" (*Black Music*, pp. 184, 185).

Baraka's music criticism and theories are his most effective pieces of writing on art. The language is generally succinct, even in rhapsodic essays like "The Changing Same," of his black nationalist period. These works on music are among the most persuasive in his essays altogether because theory and conclusion alike are often linked with demonstrable facts. The theoretical statement, however questionable its implications might be, is integrated with the concrete; and even the dogmatic assertion gains a certain plausibility by virtue of Baraka's obvious knowledge and love of his subject. There is consequently a compelling force in the essay on Thelonius Monk because the precise description of Monk's style (from piano technique to improvised dance steps) really authenticates a recurrent Baraka thesis: that black music is a total experience, that the performer's environment, the musical form itself, and the attendant feelings are all fused into one whole.

By a similar token the description of black music as "unity" music and as the expression of black spirituality rests on the historical facts of the black church's pervasive influence on all major aspects of black American life. And on this basis "The Changing Same" allows Baraka to integrate his aesthetic approach to black music with the tightly knit dialectic of the black nationalist's "operational unity" (*Black Music*, p. 210). This success is only a qualified one. Despite a certain measure of historical justification, his aesthetics of black "unity" music suffer from the dogmatic narrowness with which he offers his black nationalist views as a whole. The contention that black music expresses a certain spirituality in black American culture is supportable enough in historical terms. But the dogmatic assertion that this spirituality is the exclusive, definitive trait of black culture and music weakens the credibility of the claim as a whole.

In the final analysis his grasp of art forms does not suffer from his insistence on the political and social significance of these forms. But it is weakened by his increasing tendency, as black aesthetician, to advance questionable distinctions between black and nonblack cultures, and to insist upon narrowly conceived, prescriptive definitions of "significance" itself. In effect Baraka the political activist (i.e., black aesthetician) destroys that very balance or synthesis between art and sociopolitical significance upon which Baraka the critic insists in earlier works like "Jazz and the White Critic" and *Blues People*.

X   *The Early Literary Criticism*

Baraka's literary criticism lacks the persuasive force of his essays on music. As literary critic he falls short of even his qualified successes in *Blues People* and *Black Music*. The single most important reason for this difference lies in Baraka's basic perception of musical and literary traditions in black America. Notwithstanding that political dogmatism that informs a concept like the idea of "unity" music, Baraka remains fairly consistent in recognizing black music as an *art* form, one that is not only politically functional and imaginatively conceived, but also legitimized by its historical relationship with the roots of the black American past. On the other hand, Baraka is never fully convinced that black American literature enjoys the integrity, as art, that he associates in these terms with black music.

This skepticism about the literature is the more pronounced because Baraka associates the artistic failures of black literature with what he perceives as moral and political bankruptcy among the educated black middle class. Hence in 1962, well before he is fully committed to black aesthetic criteria, "The Myth of a 'Negro Literature' " compares black literature unfavorably with black music, designating the latter as the expression of "the black man's soul," and scorning the former as superficially "cultivated" middle-class attempts to imitate white literary models. The literature therefore fails Baraka's standards of serious art, those standards by which he judges black music as expressive form: "High art . . . must issue from

real categories of human activity, *truthful* accounts of human life"
(*Home*, pp. 106–107, 109). This conviction that the literature lacks
the imaginative dimensions of "serious" art forms like black music
seems to encourage a certain prescriptiveness, especially after 1963:
on the whole he tends to define the ideal black writer simply as
political activist while it is the musician who emerges again and again
in these latter essays as the archetype of the ideal black artist, one
whose forms are both politically significant and imaginatively conceived.

The problem is not that Baraka criticizes mediocrity as such in
black American literature, but that he never really ever seems willing
to demonstrate that the literature can and sometimes does offer
examples of literary modes as imaginative, committed art forms. As
we shall see, his own work as literary artist is motivated by a deep-
seated interest in the possibilities of literature as ethnically committed, imaginatively structured art forms—despite his hostility to the
Western models of his literary forms. But he is able to pursue this
interest because he legitimizes his literary art by associating it, in a
variety of ways, with the oral traditions of black American culture and
with that musical tradition which he recognizes as the only true art
form to evolve from the black American experience.

However, this strategy does not really influence his approach, as
critic, to black American literature. His class bias is also significant
here. Thus black music is a valid art form not only because it expresses "the black man's soul," but also because it proceeds from the
souls of the black poor and the black working class—from the "roots."
Literature, on the other hand, is the product of an educated middle-
class group whose education encourages a cultural imitativeness
rather than imaginative freshness. In light of all this it is possible to
link "The Myth of a 'Negro Literature' " with the black aesthetic of
later years. There is a tendency here to define the "authenticity" of
black literature on wholly sociological or political grounds rather than
as politically significant art. The essay may also be viewed as an early
progenitor of the development which eventually leads Baraka to
scientific socialism: the bias here against the "Negro" middle class is
really not different in kind from subsequent contempt for the shallow-
ness and opportunism of the "black petite bourgeoisie."

XI   *The Black Aesthetic and Literary Criticism*

This fundamental skepticism about the possibilities of black literature fosters the uniform abusiveness and general prescriptiveness

with which Baraka approaches the subject of black writing. Consequently "Brief Reflections on Two Hot Shots" (1963) has very little to say about the actual achievements of South Africa's Peter Abrahams or America's James Baldwin as black novelists. It is a continuous racial diatribe that dismisses both writers as novelists because the critic has determined that they really wish to be white (*Home*, p. 120). But this does not really come to terms with the manifold issues raised by the art of someone like Baldwin, particularly when the novelist's work demands attention as a valid reflection of certain black American realities—however much these realities might contradict the ideals of black unity and black pride.

But these earlier essays on black literature are not a total failure. Like many of his fellow black aestheticians Baraka is on surer ground, and therefore more convincing, when his "aesthetics" take the form of protesting the limitations of traditional academic criticism of the literature. "Hunting Is Not Those Heads on the Wall" (1964) is an example of this strength: "The academic Western mind is the best example of the substitution of artifact worship for the lightning awareness of the art process. . . . The academician, the aesthete, are like deists whose specific corruption of mysticism is to worship things" (*Home*, p. 174). In other words, academic preoccupation with literary form has led to the neglect of literary art as statement.

On the whole, however, Baraka's literary criticism becomes progressively prescriptive as it is more fully integrated with the Black Arts Movement. "State/meant" (1965) is typical of the style and sentiments of the black aesthetic in Baraka's literary criticism. Like the black nationalist rhetoric of which it is a part his literary criticism is now a combination of bombast and abuse: the black artist's role is to "aid in the destruction of America as he knows it," to make black men strong and white men mad (*Home*, p. 251). And in "The Revolutionary Theatre" (1964) Baraka enthuses over his own vision of "twenty million spooks storming America with furious cries and unstoppable weapons" (*Home*, p. 214).

The exhortation and the political pun in the title of "State/meant" emphasize that functionalism which, typically, integrates artistic statement with the politics of state, and which will persist through to the socialist views of more recent years. And it is also typical that this ideal integration of literature and politics complements Baraka's philosophical ideal of cosmic wholeness. Hence in "The Revolutionary Theatre" the black dramatist should, ideally, force social change by encouraging the reconciliation of rational and spiritual values in the society. As with "unity" music the dialectic of wholeness applies to the *nature* of revolutionary theater (the functional integration of politics and art) as equally as it does to the political goals themselves. This dialectic allows Baraka the only basis on which he seems able to treat literary art and political change interchangeably. He does this in "The Fire Must Be Permitted to Burn Full Up" (*Raise*, pp. 117–23), as well as in his famous poem "Black Art," in which the black poem and the new black nation are, ideally, one indivisible whole.[15]

But even this concession to literature as a potentially committed art form is largely in the area of drama. Although the advocacy of literary art as political commitment apparently encompasses black literature as a whole, it is really the theater that attracts Baraka whenever he chooses to elaborate on the subject—whether he is advocating theater as a revolutionary force ("The Revolutionary Theatre") or whether he is lambasting black dramatists, as he does in the introduction to his play *Jello* (1970), for betraying the ideal of commitment. And in this regard it is significant that, as we shall see in due course, both his theories and practice as socialist writer are centered primarily on the theater.

Baraka appears to be more comfortable with theater in this regard because it is an art form that seems peculiarly practical as political tool. Here he is dealing with a form that attracts him by virtue of those nonverbal elements (spectacle, dance, music, action, and so forth) which result in less dependence on the literary word. Dramatic action, whether in full-fledged, complex plays or in agit-prop pieces, attracts him because it is both microcosm and symbol of his political activism. And as we shall see in the study of his own plays, theater accommodates his needs as activist by facilitating the need to complement language with action; it therefore offers the opportunity to synthesize *literary* forms with political ideas; and in accomplishing or promising all of this it fulfils that ideal of wholeness which remains central to Baraka's idealism as critic and political writer.

CHAPTER 3

Baraka as Novelist:
The System of Dante's Hell

I *Baraka and the Novel*

BARAKA'S skepticism about the achievement of black American literature is most profound when he contemplates the black novel. As we have already noted, he associates black literature (including the novel) with an educated middle class whose preference for the genre reflects a certain self-destructive fascination with the white culture that is the source of genres like the novel (*Home*, pp. 105–15). In light of this skepticism it is significant that his only novel was written and published (1965) before the full development of his black aesthetic views made him even more hostile to art forms (especially the novel) which seemed indelibly Western (that is, nonblack) by virtue of their sources and evolution. And it is not surprising that his own novel reflects a certain determination to avoid that derivativeness which, in his opinion, has been the bane of the black novel in America.

Consequently all of those features of *The System of Dante's Hell* which have puzzled or exasperated some critics result from a deep ambivalence on Baraka's part toward the genre. The use of nonstandard English, the exploitation of jazz and blues idioms, the reliance on series of images rather than descriptive narration, the evocation of the spoken word, and the disdain for conventional narrative sequence—all of these features reflect Baraka's unresolved but intrinsically creative conflict with the novel as both literary genre and cultural symbol. Of course there is nothing unique in Baraka's subversive sense of form within his chosen genre. The history of the novel offers numerous parallels to the kind of ambivalence which he experiences.

But these tensions assume a special significance in Baraka's case because so much of his conflict with the fictive form is bound up with

the manner in which he perceives art and America as a whole. As a
European import the novel can never compete with jazz or the blues
as a peculiarly American medium rooted in the history and ethnic
experiences of America. In a sense the novel therefore represents
America's resilient colonial heritage. Consequently most black fiction
is merely the imitation of an imitation.[1] Baraka's own novel must
therefore be perceived not simply as a novel but also as an assault
upon the form itself. The assault takes the form of violent language
and the jettisoning of any predefined narrative order. And it also
represents both Baraka's rebellion against the black novelist's traditional imitativeness and, in broader terms, the apparent subservi-
ence of the American novel to European tradition.

On this basis, then, the idea of fictive form has special significance
in Baraka's novel. Form is central to his theme of ethnic growth and
rebellion in white American culture. The apparent vagaries and
eccentricities of form reflect a continuing tension between the artist
and his genre; but at the same time that tension is internalized,
dramatizing the self-conflicts that are central to the novel's ethnic
figures. Furthermore the tension between black ethnicity—the
novel's main theme—and the idea of fictive form implies a conflict of
sorts between content and form. But such a "conflict" is not an ideal,
as his essays on politics and art should have already demonstrated. On
the contrary it actually confirms his ideal of wholeness or moral
integration precisely because the struggle between ethnic theme and
borrowed Western form is a satiric reminder of fragmentation and
divisiveness within the novelist's culture. In short, the very sense of a
conflict between fictive form and moral experience reinforces
Baraka's insistence, in his aesthetics and in his political ideology, on
an ethos of unity or wholeness.

It is necessary to emphasize the implications of Baraka's narrative
form and his perception of the novel as a genre, because these
implications, together with the undeniable difficulties of the work,
explain its curious neglect in the study of the novel in America. One
recent critic actually dismisses it as "an expressionistic, semi-
autobiographical, semi-pornographic prose thing."[2] And, in the
words of another critic, the novel is merely "experimental," and is as
"explosive and directionless as some of Jones's poems."[3] The condescending description of the novel as "experimental" is curiously
perverse because its innovativeness is in fact one of its main
strengths, especially in its adaptation of black American media
(speech and music, for example) to the Euro-American literary genre.

Moreover, quite apart from the special difficulties posed by Baraka's novel, the study of his work has suffered from a general tendency in traditional criticism, to dissociate style or technique from thematic content. Several years ago Mark Schorer lamented this shortcoming in terms which have important implications for the study of novels in general but which are also a blueprint of sorts for any satisfactory approach to the relationship between style and content in *The System of Dante's Hell*: "As for the resources of language; these, somehow, we almost never think of as a part of the technique of fiction—language as used to create a certain texture and tone which in themselves state and define themes and meanings; or language, the centers of our ordinary speech, as forced through conscious manipulation, into all those larger meanings which our speech almost never intends." [4]

Here too we may note yet another example of the manner in which Baraka's intellectual rebellion against the white West is supported by elements of Western thought and criticism. And this leads to a logical parallel: the novel as a Western-derived form becomes a weapon of rebellion against the novel and its Western cultural sources, in much the same way that the novel's rebelliously anti-Western synthesis of form and meaning fulfills at least one major aspect of Western literary scholarship. Baraka's modes of rebellion, in this novel as well as in the essays that we have already examined, are often as significant in delineating his Western, American heritage as they are in expressing an explicit rejection of that heritage.

That explicit rejection is the main, more obvious burden of *The System of Dante's Hell*. Given Baraka's subversive view of narrative plot as fictive convention, it is not surprising that the "plot" of the work is rather slight. It centers on the life of Roi, alternately identified as Dante, beginning with his life in the black ghetto of Newark. This ghetto phase occupies more than half of the novel and is described by way of multiple images (conveying the sights, sounds, and emotional texture of Roi's world) rather than by way of episodes. This section of the novel creates general impressions of Roi's environment; and at the same time the impression of a destructive yet intensely vital world serves to focus the reader's attention on the specific personalities of Roi and his circle, as well as on Roi's changing perception of the world around him.

Roi's education and career as air force recruit take him farther from the black community and closer to the social and intellectual milieu of white America. This development has ambiguous results. On the one hand, the escape from the socioeconomic "hell" of the black slum is understandable. But on the other hand, it is an attempt to flee from self, from his racial identity and cultural roots—into the hellish milieu of a hostile white world whose literature, money, and institutions excercise a powerful influence. Roi's early experience is therefore an allegory of sorts, dramatizing a central dilemma in the black American experience. The decay and the destructive violence of the slum encourages the inevitable need to escape into relative middle-class comfort. But the black ghetto is not a mere slum. It is also a community with a distinctive life-style and with patterns of language, music, and social codes that distinguish it as a cultural milieu. And as a vital community it still represents crucial values even to those who escape. Moreover, since even this distinctive culture exists as part of (rather than apart from) America in Baraka's prenationalist writings, then Roi's fundamental problem is to retain the positive values of his black community while functioning, as he must, as an American in America.

The problem is never fully resolved in the novel. The latter half of the work gradually shifts from the multiple images of the first half. In a series of progressively "narrative" episodes we witness Roi's gradual rejection of the white world, or at the very least that aspect of white perception which encourages black self-hatred. Conversely, this kind of rejection goes hand in hand with attempts to affirm his racial identity. The setting for the most crucial of these attempts is the Bottom, a Southern black ghetto. The ghetto itself is similar to the Newark slum of his past, but the name emphasizes his own personal changes: he has sunk to the bottom of his hell of racial self-rejection. He is now an "imitation" white boy and his visit is a kind of pilgrimage, a perverse pilgrimage consciously dedicated to the denial of his ethnicity. His sexual failure with Peaches, a black prostitute, therefore represents his failure as a human being. And this broader failure is underscored by Peaches's personality—a tough-minded commitment to her private and racial integrity, and a degree of self-knowledge that is the antithesis of Roi's self-hating habit of denying any fellowship with other blacks.

Before he leaves Peaches he does learn to share and appreciate her world. He "felt the world grow together as I hadn't known it. All lies before, I thought. All fraud and sickness. This was the world. It leaned under its own suns, and people moved on it. A real world, of flesh, of smells, of soft black harmonies and color. The dead maelstrom of my head, a sickness" (p. 148).[5] But this sharing is only temporary. He must eventually return to the air force and the white world in which he functions. The affirmation of his blackness and the rejection of his imitation whiteness are not complete when the novel ends; but at the very least there has been a fundamental new beginning in which Roi has begun to evaluate his hybrid heritage and identity as a black American.

II   *Baraka and His Western Literary Heritage*

The autobiographical parallels between Baraka's own life and the plot of his novel are inescapable, especially when we bear in mind the protagonist's name, his Newark background, his service in the United States Air Force, and his aspirations to be a writer. And Baraka's own postcript to the work reinforces these parallels by summarizing the theme as his interpretation of his earlier life (p. 153). The period in which this interpretation took place ("around 1960–1961") is significant. For what is most important here is not the extent to which the novel fictionalizes Baraka's life as such, but the manner in which the themes of ethnic identity reflect Baraka's own ambivalence, at this period, toward his Western intellectual heritage.

Consequently, notwithstanding the eventual date of publication (1965), *The System of Dante's Hell* represents much of Baraka's earliest self-perception as artist. The choice of a genre which he views as the black writer's Western badge indicates that this period of "interpretation" was also one in which the Western heritage exercised enormous influence on the conscious workings of his intellectuality and artistic imagination. And in turn the very force of that influence was already beginning to provoke an ethnic reaction within Baraka the artist. But despite that reaction the Western influence remains evident in the literary allusions to a host of Western writers and philosophers. The Western heritage also deserves careful examination because Baraka's statements seem, at times, to repudiate that heritage in its entirety. For when the very act of repudiation dominates a work like *Dante's Hell* it underscores the continuing influence (negative or otherwise) on the artist himself. The conscious act of repudiation does not constitute an expunging: the philosophical habits and technical skills that Baraka develops under the Western influence have not disappeared simply because he questions aspects of Western culture and art.

Dante's Hell is very appropriate here because quite apart from the obvious reference to Dante Alighieri's *Inferno* Baraka's novel is

saturated with allusions to major Western writers from Homer to
Eliot. Moreover, the novel is a sustained dramatization of the continuing ambiguities that are inherent in the relationship between
Baraka and his literary heritage. The allusive texture of the narrative
is amply demonstrated by Roi's initial impressions of a brothel in the
Bottom: "He pointed like Odysseus and like Virgil, the weary shade,
at some circle. For Dante, me, the young wild virgin of the universe
to look. To see what terror. What illusion. What sudden shame, the
world is made. Of what death and lust I fondled and thot to make
beautiful or escape, at least, into some other light, where each death
was abstract and intimate" (p. 126).

This brief introduction to the brothel scene juxtaposes allusions to
the Ulysses archetype in Homer (*The Odyssey*) and Dante (*The
Inferno*, in which Virgil guides the poet to hell), and Tennyson's "The
Lotus-Eaters," where Ulysses points the way to his travel-worn crew.
The allusions also include James Joyce's *Ulysses* (the entry of the
"virginal" young poet into a brothel—a parallel that is subsequently
reinforced by Roi's reference to himself by the Joycean name,
Stephen Dedalus). Finally the literary allusions are interwoven with
the mythic reference in that the echoes of the Joycean hero recall the
legend of another artist-creator, the mythical Daedalus. The remark-
ably compact nature of these multiple allusions is important. The
form and structure of these compacted allusions constitute a telescop-
ing effect, the kind of historical perspective that enables us to perceive the Ulysses archetype, simultaneously, in a succession of
epochs in literature, from Homer to Joyce. The passage as a whole
therefore offers an archetypal perspective on the very (literary) tradition with which Baraka interacts throughout his novel.

Once again, this interaction is based on Baraka's ambivalence
toward his Western heritage. Thus in perceiving the literary tradition
behind the Ulysses archetype Roi identifies himself with Dante and
with Joyce's Dedalus. In Dante's *Inferno* Ulysses' passionate quest
for knowledge and for the complete experience of life itself demands
our admiration, in much the same way that Tennyson's Ulysses (in
both "The Lotus-Eaters" and "Ulysses") commands our respect. But
Dante's Ulysses is predominantly a figure of sin, the sin of pursuing
knowledge egotistically, to the neglect of family and social responsi-
bilities. Joyce's Ulysses archetype, Leopold Bloom, is a sympathetic
figure of compassion and humanity; but Stephen Dedalus the young
poet is his antithesis, the detached artist-intellectual as opposed to
the warm, involved Bloom. In identifying Roi with Dedalus and with

Dante's Ulysses, then, Baraka evokes critical response to the archetype insofar as Ulysses represents a single-minded pursuit of knowledge.

Moreover this implied detachment emphasizes Roi's inadequacy in the kind of humanity that the Joycean Ulysses (Bloom) symbolizes—and in specifically ethnic terms this stresses Roi's limited self-image as a black. But in another sense Roi is also Ulysses, for, as the symbol of the quest for knowledge and for an expanded consciousness, the Ulysses figure represents Roi's odyssey for human and ethnic wholeness in the novel; and as such the archetype promises a capacity for growth even in Roi's most limited moments in the novel. This ambivalence toward the Ulysses archetype forms a basic irony in Baraka's novel. Since the archetype represents not only growth and knowledge as such but also those Western intellectual traditions that have influenced the young Roi, then the maturing of Roi's ethnic sensibilities depends on some detachment from the culture represented by the archetype.

The irony of developing a black odyssey in order to disengage his hero from Ulysses' Western culture is complemented by Baraka's basic strategy: he identifies his art with the literary symbols of the West (Dante and Dedalus) in order to disengage himself from the literary and philosophical traditions of the West. And, by extension, Roi's ambivalence toward white America reflects Baraka's treatment of the West in the novel as a whole. The Western heritage is deeply suspect but its influence is persuasive, precisely because it is the source of so many of the referents that are available, even indispensable, to the black artist who is attempting to define his own sense of identity and tradition.

In effect, Western history and the novelist's own past embody ethnocultural values which not only subvert or threaten black self-acceptance, but are also intertwined with the roots of his art. Consequently, the very act of attempting to counter that subversiveness attests to the persuasiveness of the Western influence on his art. That influence is implied by the large number of references to Western writers, especially to Dante, T. S. Eliot, Joyce, and the existentialists.

III   *Baraka and Dante*

Of these Dante's relationship with Baraka's novel is the most immediate. The parallels between *The Inferno* and the themes of

Dante's Hell are fairly accessible despite the complaint by one critic that the relationship between the two works is merely casual.[6] The main effect of Baraka's adaptation of *The Inferno* is the emphasis on his rejection of the Christian image of hell and of the religious morality on which that image is based. From Baraka's viewpoint the "hell" of Western literature and Christian thought is a myth that reflects the culture's ingrained habits of establishing dichotomies between feeling and reason, spirit and matter, social experience and religious systems. The "hell" that does provoke his urgent concern is not definable in terms of Christian mythology or in the terms upon which Dante's work uses that mythology. It exists as a continuing social reality: it represents Western modes of perception which arbitrarily distinguish between races, between feeling and reason, and which constitute a kind of hell for their victims. "Hell" is Baraka's synonym for social systems and ideologies that destroy the spirit and the mind by distorting human needs and values. Consequently, hell is definable, for Baraka, only in social terms. It is "in the head," in ethnic terms, for those blacks who are "unfocused" on their racial identity (p. 153).

In effect, Baraka has transformed the Christian's mythic image of hell into the everyday realities of social, racial, and moral divisiveness—into the "flame of social dichotomy" (p. 153). Of course Dante does invest his own inferno with the dimensions of everyday reality by allegorically exploring the social ramifications of his characters' sins. But notwithstanding this social dimension the underlying concepts of sin versus innocence, heaven versus hell are still conventionally Christian and, therefore, substantially different in kind from Baraka's perception. Dante explores historical and social experiences by using an accepted body of Christian doctrine and myths. On the other hand Baraka probes his own social experience by redefining or demolishing the symbols of existing systems—including the religious and moral systems that are fundamental to the moral viewpoint of a writer like Dante. Hence the relationship between Baraka's novel and Dante's poem is not merely "casual," but *causal* in an intensely satiric and reactional sense.

In this regard *Dante's Hell* is, in part, a satire of that Western need to systematize experience, a need that seems to be represented by Dante's *Inferno*, complete with its highly complex structure of paganism and piety, sins and circles. From the viewpoint of *Dante's Hell* Dante's *Inferno* depicts hell in terms of that abstract morality which Baraka associates with the abstractionism of Western thought as a whole. It is another example, Baraka observes, of the manner in which a rationalistic society—a "world of technology"—demands ethical systems that are suitable to its ingrained rationalism (p. 98). And as a limited form of perception the abstract rationalism represented by Dante's Christianity is particularly destructive to blacks who are assimilated into white culture—particularly since the black-versus-white symbolism of white culture often reinforces the ethos of white superiority (white as good) as opposed to black inferiority (black as evil).

In addition to the philosophical implications and racial parallels that Baraka examines in the white, Christian vision of hell, he is also interested in the idea of hell as a socioeconomic reality spawned by white racism and by American institutions. On this level hell is the violence and decay of the black ghetto. And in making this point, Baraka evokes a deep-seated and disturbing sense of absurdity: the everyday hell of the black ghetto reduces the Christian hell to a certain level of relative insignificance. When men storm a building, in a blind, unexplained rage, in order to kill some unindentified "muthafucka," then we are left with indelible impressions of a "hell" which is deadly precisely because it is so much a part of everyday routine, and which is absurd because it is actually an extension of a "Christian" society that has managed to compile elaborate, metaphysical images of hell while creating and ignoring another kind of hell in its midst (p. 99).

In the light of all this, in the face of all those half-crazed, would-be killers, metaphysical image-makers like Dante seem merely effete, even obscure, in the "loveliness" of their abstract, moral systems: "Lovely Dante at night under his flame taking heaven. A place, a system, where all is dealt with . . . as is proper" (p. 99). In short, Christian idealism and its associated (Dantesque) symbols are really a kind of escape from the world that Baraka forces to our attention. "Lovely" Dante therefore embodies the evasiveness that Baraka attributes here to Western ethics and literature. And the archetypal figure of the poet is simultaneously identified with Roi, whose escapism is twofold. It is cultural, by virtue of his adaptation of those Western value systems which he acquires in graduating from ghetto life. And it is physical—the flame (marijuana, presumably) that brings a temporary "heaven" from the hell of the ghetto and from his private hell of becoming "unfocused" on his blackness. In the "real" hell of Roi's world, Dante's "heaven" is reduced, with calculating absurdity, to a rather cheap and easy vision of escape.

This kind of irony is complemented by another, in Baraka's response to the idea of the Christian's hell. From a certain perspective the "hell" of the black ghetto is also a kind of heaven: "Dante's hell is heaven. Look at things in another light" (p. 9). For although the slum is partly a hellish environment spawned by the hellish systems outside, it also includes a human vitality that has defied the law and order of scientific logic by the sheer fact that it has survived in such circumstances. The black ghetto therefore bears all the cruel signs of despoilation side by side with a defiant sense of life. And, to continue the thread of Baraka's thematic irony, this vitalism in the midst of the black urban wasteland is a kind of absurdity, a triumphant absurdity it is true, but one that contradicts the strictly "logical" viewpoints that are so important in the white world outside the ghetto.

Moreover, when we turn from the general idea of hell to the circles of hell which Baraka borrows from Dante we find that here too Baraka has invested the original material with the ironies of his satiric vision. This vision is illustrated quite well by three representative sections: the Vestibule, Circle One (heathen), and Circle Seven (hypocrites). Dante's original Vestibule is occupied by the futile, the souls of those who lacked moral purpose and judgment in their lives. But the occupants of Baraka's Vestibule are called "neutrals." The label intensifies the original image of fence-straddling and moral aimlessness which mark the futile opportunists of Dante's *Inferno*. Baraka's neutrals are not simply displaced and aimless beings. They are, by virtue of that moral emptiness, merely things.

Moreover Baraka intensifies the satiric significance of Dante's Vestibule by extending the connotations of neutrality beyond the context of ethical choices. A neutral in *Dante's Hell* is a thing because his human sensibility has been shattered (p. 9). And in addition to all of this, the neutral is a mere thing when that neutral is a black person in a white world that perceives blacks as things anyway and accepts that subhuman definition of his or her ethnicity. The social consequences of this ethnic "neutrality" intensify the condition of being a mere thing. The special socioeconomic determinism of the black ghetto, with its built-in cycles of poverty and crime, deprives blacks of meaningful choices. And in this sense they are also the victims of an imposed neutrality: they must either remain prisoners of the Vestibule-ghetto, or they must assimilate themselves into the white world outside at the cost of denying their ethnic integrity.

In light of all this the term "neutrals" acquires multiple connotations in Baraka's "Vestibule" section. It represents black self-hatred, the "break-up" of black sensibility. It describes the white world's perception of blacks as things, as minds of darkness. The term reflects the lifelessness of an environment in which the denial of black humanity (by blacks and whites alike) allows the mind to be interchangeable with "things" like rotting vegetables, dogs, and chipped stone stairs. And it reinforces a sense of moral emptiness that reduces the echoes of an age-old idealism (Justice, Egalité) to the level of mere traffic noise (p. 9).

As for the heathens of the first circle, Baraka dissociates his narrative definition of heathenism from Dante's even as he exploits Dante's moral and narrative structures. In *The Inferno* the virtuous heathen are barred from heaven because they did not receive Christian baptism, but are spared from hell because of their natural virtues. But in *Dante's Hell* the notion of exclusion and semiadmittance has been transformed from a moral issue to a socioeconomic one. Baraka's heathens are, therefore, the lower middle class—too poor to participate in the "heaven" of the American Dream, too affluent, in relative terms, to be numbered with the dregs of the ghetto. Despised by those above and below, the lower-middle-class individual is linked to the neutrals by the impression of being a mere object in the social scheme of things, especially in a success-oriented society in which failure is unforgivable.

The Baraka heathen is therefore defined by the empty and dirty *things* which clutter up the character's immediate surroundings—an empty glass on an ugly dining-room table, a burning cigarette, the clutter of old letters, discarded magazines and old books, together with a floor that crawls with roaches nibbling on stale food particles. Baraka's careful attention to descriptive detail emphasizes this interchangeability of the inanimate and the human in the emotional and socioeconomic limbo of the heathen's world. The empty glass is complemented by mental sogginess and emptiness. In turn, the emptiness of mind is ironically counterbalanced by the "full" floor of dirt and by the repulsive clutter of the room. Lastly, the tell-tale signs of age and usage appear equally in the surrounding objects and in the weary sogginess of the heathen's eyes. Like the neutral, the heathen is the finished product, or thing, of surrounding systems (p. 13).

The hypocrites of the eighth circle are also reflections of the society in which the novelist locates them. Here too Baraka redefines and supplements the familiar (Christian) connotations of Dante's originals. Dante's hypocrites are, conventionally, obvious symbols of deliberate deception. But the concept of hypocrisy assumes additional connotations in *Dante's Hell*. Here Baraka has also presented the experience of hypocrisy as a kind of fear, one that has been inspired by the violence and general tone of the city. The environment in which Baraka's hypocrites move—they are actually black church-worshipers—leaves them with the choice of shouting or stealing. The conventional connotations of hypocrisy are clear enough in the smiles of the church trustees (after they have taken in the money) or in the suspect saintliness of easy tears among the worshipers. But the narrative description of the hypocrites moves beyond this level.

The hypocrisy that Baraka attributes to fear here is not merely a deliberate religious sham. On a conscious level piety is really a genuinely felt religious experience. But on another level this experience is really a kind of escape. Baraka's black saints are fanatically devoted to their church because they are afraid of an outside world with which they cannot cope. This is the world of the streets. And in addition to this fearful escape from the social environment there is the crucial issue of escaping from one's self, from the realities of one's deepest impulses and desires: like James Baldwin, Baraka is noting that the saint's religious zeal is in direct proportion to a suppressed or conscious fascination with the "sins" of the street.[7] Consequently the choice between shouting or stealing is more than an option *within* the church itself—that is, the option of being a shouting saint or an exploitive church official. It is also the choice, or seeming choice, between the church itself and the world outside. In turn, the hypocrite's false choices, between the destructiveness of the streets and the self-delusions of the church, recall the nonexistent or meaningless choices in the experiences of both the neutrals and the heathens. Once again, as he carefully redefines the Dantesque symbols with which he works Baraka establishes a sense of narrative and thematic unities by virtue of that sociopolitical perspective which informs his adaptation of Dante's *Inferno*.

Altogether Baraka has transferred Dante's hell, complete with its circular schema, from the moral definitions of Western Christianity to the everyday realities of black America's twentieth-century ghettoes. In so doing he has transformed that hell into a symbol of white perception, black self-images, and the social environment as a whole. At the same time he is able to subvert Dante's underlying Christian morality by interpreting it as part of that systematizing tradition which has spawned a variety of social hells in Western culture. And Baraka achieves this in the very process of imitating Dante's undeniable achievement—of using hell as a mirror of social types and historical events. For despite the ethical gulf between them, it is clear that Dante's hell is not simply a religious allegory but also a concretely social one; and Baraka's subversion of Dante's moral and religious schema is therefore intensified by the very degree to which Dante actually provides him with the model of using hell as social mirror.

Baraka's detachment from the moral conventions of that model also influences the thematic and structural relationships between the circles of his hell. In *Dante's Hell* we are not really conscious of that sense of moral degeneration which defines the inverted hierarchy of Dante's *Inferno*. As we have already noted in the examples of the neutrals, heathens and hypocrites, the circles of Baraka's hell are linked along a horizontal, rather than hierarchical, plane: no one group is "morally worse" than the other. The point is to explore the connections and similarities between them as products of the same system, and to dramatize the manner in which that exploration eventually shapes Roi's evolving consciousness.

This is not, of course, to deny that there is a "progression" or (from another viewpoint) "degeneration" in the novel's structure. On another plane there are vertical connections between the circles of Baraka's hell. But here again the contrast with the Dante model is illuminating. The hierarchical structure of the Dante original is there for the hero to observe as he travels from the Vestibule down to the very bottom of hell itself, from the innocuous neutrals to Satan himself. On the other hand, the quality of life in Baraka's ghetto-life remains quite uniform throughout. It is the evolution of Roi's personality that creates the impression of a descent. Roi's changing relationship with the ghetto and with black life in general constitutes an estrangement from his black identity and culture. It therefore represents a continuing descent into the subjective hell of his consciousness.

Baraka's estrangement from the established conventions which shape Dante's vision of hell as a fixed hierarchy is further emphasized by another aspect of Baraka's hell. The novelist departs, in a major instance, from Dante's original sequence of circles. As he explains in his preface he places heretics in the deepest part of his hell, unlike Dante who placed them on higher ground. He effects this change by insisting on the definition of heresy in social and psychological terms: it represents the flight from one's roots and self; it is the denial of feeling; and in this sense it is the greatest of "evils." The definition of heresy in these terms and the narrative structure which evolves from it rest on Roi's subjective experience (his relationship with his self-hood and ethnic sources), rather than on a preexisting moral schema sanctioned by established religious convention. And in Baraka's subjective context the "bottom" of hell has no meaning outside the consciousness of the narrator-protagonist, Roi. It symbolizes the depth of his self-hatred. Consequently, that "vertical" connection between the circles of Baraka's hell reflects the hero's plunge into the "basest evil" (p. 7) of self-hate.

IV   *Baraka and T. S. Eliot*

Baraka's ambiguous relationship with *The Inferno* as his model and his novel's antithesis leads to the issue of his awareness of his art in time and tradition. That is, Baraka's handling of Dante and other models reflects a certain preoccupation with the nature of the links between (Western) literary tradition as such and his individual talent as a black writer. And on this basis there are clear parallels between Baraka's novel and T. S. Eliot's description of the relationship between the artist and the tradition within which that artist creates. Hence, to return to the Ulysses archetype in *Dante's Hell*, Baraka derives a certain sense of simultaneity from the use of archetypal figures because the ages-old sources of the archetype allows the writer to synthesize past and present in one moment. And this kind of simultaneity is similar in kind to that historical perspective which Eliot describes in his essay "Tradition and the Individual Talent": "The historical sense involves a perception, not only of the pastness of the past, but of its presence; the historical sense compels a man to write not only with his own generation in his bones, but with a feeling that the whole of the literature of Europe . . . [and] the whole of the literature of his own country has a simultaneous existence and composes a simultaneous order. This historical sense . . . makes a writer most acutely conscious of his place in time, of his own contemporaneity." [8]

The Ulyssess archetype that we have noted in *Dante's Hell* exemplifies Eliot's argument in that the archetypal mode reflects Baraka's simultaneous perception of past and present. The archetypal method also reflects his awareness of the nature of his relationship with the long literary tradition that is represented by the Ulysses archetype itself, from Homer to the modern period. And within the novel itself the protagonist Roi is "acutely conscious" of his ethnic and cultural "contemporaneity" in American society, first on the basis of an imitation whiteness, then on the basis of an emerging racial conscience. Moreover, like his creator, Roi recognizes the coexistence of the "presence" and "pastness" of Western cultural tradition. This recognition is implicit in the fact that he perceives his identity in relation to the major representatives of that tradition, and that when he subsequently embarks on his own odyssey for ethnic wholeness and integrity the Ulysses archetype that once symbolized his "white" Western traditions now represents a quest for ethnic identity.

While Eliot's essay sheds light on the significance of tradition and individual experience in *Dante's Hell*, his other critical works also illuminate another specific aspect of Baraka's response to Western literature. Hence there are informative parallels between Baraka's ambivalence toward Dante and Eliot's qualified acceptance of *The Inferno*. Baraka accepts some of Dante's themes and narrative details while rejecting the underlying Christian mythology of *The Inferno*. In his essay "Dante," Eliot enjoys the total effect of Dante's poetic imagination while lacking any real enthusiasm for Dante's dogma: "I deny that the reader must share the beliefs of the poet in order to enjoy the poetry fully" (*Selected Essays*, p. 255). Or in the words of another critic, although Dante's Christian viewpoint would lose its unity and vitality among Dante's successors, "the European mind was so permeated with the idea of human destiny that even in very un-Christian artists it preserved the Christian force and tension which were Dante's gift to posterity." [9]

These latter observations apply equally well to the Anglo-Catholic Eliot and to the decidedly anti-Christian Baraka insofar as they emphasize a certain level of ambivalence toward Dante's art. And, equally significant, this kind of ambivalence is manifest in the manner in which Baraka views Eliot himself in *Dante's Hell*. His sense of tradition and his qualified enthusiasm for Dante's art suggest that Baraka's themes have been influenced by Eliot's work, or at the very least, by the kind of intellectual criteria which Eliot contributed to modern criticism. On this basis Baraka's novel as a whole is an extension of that affinity which his protagonist Roi feels for Eliot and other Western artists. Roi identifies Eliot, Pound, and Cummings as members of his neighborhood, as parts of an erudite youth that was also marked by a sexual preference for light-skinned girls. But even in the process of establishing that affinity between his intellectual growth and white Western artists Roi admits to a certain self-destructiveness. The sexual preference that he describes in the same context suggests racial self-hatred. And that context therefore imparts a certain ambiguity to this tribute to the Western heritage: Eliot and others have been crucial to his intellectual growth, but in retrospect they are also part of those Western values which he has perverted into a "light-skinned" denial of his racial identity.

This implied detachment from Eliot is more explicit as Roi is progressively forced to deal with his racial "heresy." As a heretic in Baraka's final circle Roi now sees his Western heritage in terms of both beauty and agony (p. 119). In that self-revealing encounter with Peaches and the black world of the Bottom, Eliot and *his* world are an alien, even subversive, irrelevance. They are now associated with a narrowly literate intelligence that seems far removed from the vital sexuality and the oral forms (language and music) of Peaches's milieu (p. 134).

Altogether, then, Baraka's relationship with both Dante and Eliot establishes his own duality as black artist. He exploits Western literary forms and traditions in order to express a growing ethnic perspective that questions, even breaks away from, Eliot's West. Having been molded by traditions represented by the Ulysses archetype, Baraka and his protagonist Roi are on an ethnic odyssey that is fostered by a deep-seated skepticism about the Western roots of his identity. But does this skepticism amount to a complete renunciation in *Dante's Hell*? Does Baraka's black odyssey imply a complete negation of the white West at this point in his career as artist? The answer seems to lie largely in the significance of James Joyce's fiction in *Dante's Hell*.

V   *Baraka and James Joyce*

By identifying Roi as another Stephen Dedalus, Baraka links the ethnic development of his protagonist with the growth of the artistic imagination as it is delineated by James Joyce in *A Portrait of the Artist as a Young Man* and in *Ulysses*. Roi's odyssey for ethnic wholeness is intensified by his simultaneous search, as artist, for a sense of moral purpose. And in this respect his experience echoes Joyce's *Ulysses*, for as we have already noted the Joycean Ulysses (Bloom) embodies the kind of sympathetic warmth that both Joyce's Stephen Dedalus and Baraka's Roi lack. Consequently Roi's development implies growth, or the possibilities of growth, into the kind of humanism embodied by Joyce's Ulysses archetype.

But here again we are confronted with the pervasive ethnocultural ambivalence that marks Baraka's novel. Baraka's Roi-Dedalus is partly modeled on Joyce's Ulysses archetype—in order to dramatize the young black's rebellion against a Western heritage that *includes* Joyce. On one level the parallels between *Dante's Hell* and *Ulysses* are clear-cut enough: Stephen Dedalus's Anglo-Irish tensions in Joyce's work are analogous to the black-white double-consciousness of Baraka's Roi-Dante-Dedalus; and the incomplete humanism of Joyce's Dedalus is duplicated in the coldness of Baraka's Roi. But in another sense, the completion of Roi's humanity and the maturity of his art depend on his ability to "break" from Joyce and his tradition (*Dante's Hell*, p. 134). Paradoxically, Roi-Dedalus can only become the humanistic Ulysses archetype—he can only realize the kind of completeness that is symbolized by the Bloom-Ulysses figure—by breaking away from the heritage that includes Joyce and the Ulysses archetype itself.

Moreover Joyce himself has perfected the kind of characterization upon which Baraka now models his protagonist. In both *A Portrait of the Artist* and *Ulysses* Stephen Dedalus's growth as an artist is influenced by a deep ambivalence toward sources (Roman Catholic, Irish, paternalistic) that are at at once formative and restrictive. In *A Portrait of the Artist* Stephen seeks intellectual wholeness by fleeing family and Ireland. The flight obviously recalls the flight of Stephen's mythic namesake, Daedalus. But it is also a reflection of Joyce's well-known theory of symbolic fatherhood, especially as that theory is expounded in *Ulysses*, where Dedalus speculates on the manner in which the child figure is a projected image of the father-artist.[10] The self-realization of the artist-son requires the negation of the father-artist's image. Stephen Dedalus's intellectual and artistic maturity depends on some negation of his family sources and cultural roots.

Baraka's Roi is modeled in part on the Joycean pattern of symbolic fatherhood insofar as his growth requires some negation of Roi's (intellectual) Western parentage. Here again the pattern of Roi's growth confirms the paradox that is fundamental to Baraka's relationship with the Western tradition: the act of negating that heritage depends, in part, on models (in this case Joycean) provided by that tradition. As Joyce's intellectual heir Baraka feels compelled to rupture the links with his literary progenitor as the very condition of his own ethnic and artistic growth. But as Joyce himself demonstrates in his own works, that very act of rupturing constitutes a recognition, even a celebration of sorts, of those ambiguous links. And to conclude the paradox, the *limits* of this breakaway in *Dante's Hell* actually recall the qualified nature of Stephen Dedalus's repudiation of his own heritage in Joyce's fiction. As students of Joyce have noted Stephen's rebellion against the Irish-Catholic heritage in *A Portrait of the Artist* does not constitute a complete break. The intellectual alienation from his religious background cannot completely expunge the kind of deep impressions which Catholicism and its ritual have left on his imagination and moral sense.[11]

In a similar vein the Joycean themes through which Baraka develops his sense of detachment from Joyce's West also demonstrate the extent to which the very process of ethnic rebellion confirms strong aesthetic and moral ties with the West, even in the act of repudiation. Consequently Baraka's Roi-Dante-Dedalus bears to the end the indelible marks of that Western influence which he inherits through Dante's moral vision, Eliot's literary criticism, and Joyce's self-consciousness as artist.

VI   *Existentialism and the Blues*

The very act of proclaiming a distinctively non-Western value system also involves the invocation of Western ideas, as well as specific authors. References to existentialist philosophy, for one, are not extensive in *Dante's Hell*, but they are not less significant for all that. The references are made in the "Eighth Ditch," a dramatic episode centering on a homosexual interlude between two boy scouts identified as "46" and "64," respectively. Number "46" is Roi-Dante, who has now become part of the black middle class, with aspirations to be a poet and with middle-American tastes for jazz at the Philharmonic. On the other hand "64" is the "underprivileged" black youth who is aggressively proud, in his own way, of that status because he has a certain pride in the cultural environment and style (in music and language, for example) of the black poor. This pride manifests itself in his insistence on being called by his name, Herman Saunders; and he is the opposite of "46," who is plagued by ethnic self-doubts and by an obsession with the "alien" language of white Americans.

Herman's homosexual seduction of "46" constitutes a kind of symbolic ritual: it represents those truths about self and experience which "46" would deny but which he is forced to acknowledge once Herman strips away his friend's middle-class respectability. Interestingly, it is the "unassimilated" Herman who actually invokes the Western tradition of existentialism, especially in relation to the philosophy of Kierkegaard. He defines his own integrity in terms of the blues—the existential blues, the blues blues, the steamshovel blues, short short blues, poetry blues, bigot blues, abstract expressionism blues, and Kierkegaard blues (pp. 185–86). Herman, the incarnation of that "pure" black expression which Baraka himself attributes to the blues tradition in *Blues People*, is in effect articulating a vision of black culture and black self-awareness in existentialist terms.

The Kierkegaard reference is central to all this. Despite his obvious sarcasm, Herman's invocation of the philosopher's name has the effect of legitimizing those subjective criteria that Baraka opposes to the cut-and-dried logic of a technological world. For it has become a truism in Kierkegaard scholarship that for Kierkegaard the subjective experience holds faith as its highest passion. And in this regard he is always opposed to the *distancing* effect of the objective perception, as opposed to the involvement of subjective experience. Moreover, Kierkegaard's insistence on the value of subjective truth always affirms the innumerable possibilities of growth, of becoming: the existent individual always feels himself or herself to be in the process of becoming or growing.[12] The philosophical argument implied by Herman's reference to Kierkegaard is therefore identical to Baraka's central thesis—the need to revolt against the rigidly objective and abstract schema in Western culture. The differences between "64"-Herman-Kierkegaard and "46"-Roi-Dante duplicate the novel's distinction between two forms of perception—the one a rigidly schematic abstractionism and the other requiring a warm, subjective involvement. Kierkegaard's ideal of subjective faith is similar in kind to the basis on which Baraka's novel defines heresy as the basest evil: heresy as the denial of feeling and self is, essentially, a reprehensible repudiation of subjectivity. Conversely, the possibilities of reclaiming one's humanity from the overly objective world of technology rest in the affirmation of subjectivity.

The subjective experience as an act of affirmation explains Baraka's insistence, through Herman, on the links between Kierkegaard and existentialism. Subjectivity as a process of affirming self is really the experience of becoming and growing. And this is the process of becoming which Jean-Paul Sartre describes as the first principle of existentialism: "Not only is man what he wills himself to be, but he is also what he wills himself to be after this thrust towards existence. . . . Man is nothing else but what he makes of himself. Such is the first principle of existentialism. It is also what is called subjectivity" (*Essays in Existentialism*, pp. 36–37).

In turn Kierkegaardian subjectivity and existentialist principles are integrated with Baraka's perception of blues. That perception is quite similar to Ellison's, notwithstanding the latter's criticism of Baraka's musical ideas in *Blues People*. In Ellison's words, the blues are not simply a musical form but a form of philosophical perception. The blues express both the agony of life and the possibility of conquering agony through "sheer toughness of spirit." They are affirmations of self, offering no "scapegoat" for the struggle with agony—except the self (*Shadow and Act*, p. 104). In effect Ellison is offering an emphasis on the blues as an example of the affirmative powers of human consciousness—the same subjective powers which Kierkegaard describes and which the modern existentialists have seen as the cornerstone of their philosophy.

On the whole, then, Baraka's invocation of Kierkegaard and the existentialists has the effect of confirming the novelist's indebtedness to the Western philosophical heritage. But paradoxically, this invocation also emphasizes the distinctive qualities of the blues as a form of perception in black America. And here again we are faced with Baraka's typical ambivalence toward his narrative forms and materials in the novel: the references to the West and the perceptions borrowed from the Western heritage serve, paradoxically, to affirm what amounts to a black American world view, as Baraka sees it. Herman, the underprivileged, uneducated young black, enjoys a "pure" (that is, ethnically authentic) expression or viewpoint which is analogous to entrenched traditions of Western philosophy. On the other hand, Roi ("46") will only be able to purge himself of his racial "heresy" by learning to integrate his borrowed Western values (as intellectual and middle-class artist) with the distinctive forms of self-affirmation that are inherent in the blues.

VII   *Theme as Structure*

The blues is not only a thematic statement in *Dante's Hell*. It also defines the structure of the novel. As a form which is in itself an expression of self-affirmation and becoming, or growth, the blues references encourage the reader to draw analogies between this theme of growth and the evolutionary form of the novel as a whole. In other words, the basic plot evolves in a manner to reflect the hero's psychic evolution, and in turn this psychic experience is interwoven with the blues as a process of self-affirmation and growth. And insofar as the unfolding of narrative plot is determined by this central theme, then the structure of the novel fulfils the insistence by some critics that form and theme should be wholly integrated, that structure should itself be a means of expression rather than simply be a vehicle for some separate, distinct thematic statement.[13]

Baraka himself is quite explicit in the work about the thematic expressiveness of his fictive structure. He describes the work as a movement from the sounds and images ("association complexes") of the first half into the straight narrative of the later sections (p. 153). The early sounds and images concentrate on the black ghetto. They constitute a kind of "disordered" associationism: ideas and scenes seem to be jumbled. This disordered structure is actually a kind of thematic statement. It confirms the disruptive violence of life in the ghetto, and at the same time the very profusion of images suggests the vitality of a living, human community beneath all of that apparent disorder. By the same token the structural progression from the chaos of these sounds and images to the "orderly" sequence of "fast" narrative implies a shift in viewpoint, a moral change within Baraka's protagonist.

The increasingly "ordered" (that is, conventional) structure of the narrative (particularly in the "Bottom" episode) reflects Roi's integration with established mainstream values. Significantly, the first major shift to relatively straightforward narrative occurs in the episode between "46" (Roi) and "64" (Herman), the episode in which Roi is for the first time forcibly confronted with his diminished humanity as an assimilated middle-class black who is ashamed of his racial identity. The narrative form of this episode takes the form of drama, and the shift in narrative technique soon takes us to conventional prose narration. For example, the story of an attempted rape by Roi and some of his friends unfolds in the ninth circle as a complete, self-contained episode—as a short story. And correspondingly this increasing emphasis on conventional prose narrative is matched by the protagonist's growing middle-class self-consciousness. He is destined, he tells us, to be a great figure in the beautiful middle class, and at this point he is capable of "treachery to kindred" (p. 107). In this instance treachery takes the form of an adolescent plot to rape a black prostitute. Unlike the earlier encounter with Herman, he is not self-defensive about his middle-class status, and he is far less likely to display sympathies for those (like the prostitute) who represent the miseries of his ghetto past. Accordingly he is the one who tries, unsuccessfully, to persist with the rape, even after his companions decide to release the woman.

When he reaches the Bottom ghetto he has arrived at the deepest part of his subjectively defined hell. He is now a confirmed heretic;

and thus the "straight" narrative becomes more pronounced, and prolonged, as it mirrors his narrowly logical and alien (white) value system. But in its total effect the Bottom does impress upon him how limited reason can be when it is divorced, as his is, from the "real" world of flesh and from his racial integrity. Consequently, as we have already seen, the end of the novel is really a kind of beginning. The hero has begun his return to humanity, from the hell of a narrow, antiblack intellectuality. On his way from Peaches's home to his air force station he is beaten by a black youth gang who hate his light skin. He eventually wakes up in a hospital, surrounded by white doctors and calling upon "God" for help. As Baraka's epilogue to the novel argues, "God" in the culture actually functions as a "white" idea. And this argument, coupled with the ethnic symbolism of the white hospital and the white air force, emphasizes the limitations of Roi's return to a black humanity at the end of the novel. But that anguished cry to "God," albeit the white idea of God, does imply that he has recognized the limited nature of his humanity as an "imitation white boy." And this implicit recognition amounts to the beginning of his progression from the hell of racial heresy.

Moreover, quite apart from the residual Christian allegiances that are inherent in that cry to God, Roi's experience at this point must also be interpreted in light of Baraka's interest in the blues and existentialism. As a blues archetype whose experience is based on the human process of "becoming" and self-affirmation, Roi also represents that subjective affirmation of self, that ability to create ourselves as we want to be, which Sartre emphasizes in his existentialist philosophy (*Essays in Existentialism*, p. 37). On this basis, then, Roi's concluding call to God is really a recognition, at last, of the godhead within, of that creatively subjective will which can allow him to make himself whatever he wants to be. On the whole, then, the echoes of the Christian deity reflect the persistence of Roi's white modes of self-perception. But on the other hand, the blues context of his entire development counterbalances those Christian implications with the ethnically self-affirmative ideas inherent in the blues tradition. Similarly, the invocation of (white) existentialist philosophy is counterbalanced by the black cultural traditions represented by the blues. And finally, this complex structure of delicately balanced meanings literally allows the conclusion of the novel to duplicate the ambiguities of Roi's experience and identity at this stage: he is an imitation white man moving toward a state of black selfhood that will be distinct from, but remain a part of, his Western milieu.

Quite apart from the manner in which it duplicates the pattern of Roi's ethnic and moral growth, the structure of the novel closely illustrates the precise details of Roi's perception and self-awareness. Both the language of the narrative summary and the plot as a whole are subordinated to Baraka's autobiographical method—that is, to the protagonist's self-description and self-analysis throughout the novel. The narrative point of view is wholly integrated with the protagonist's awareness within this autobiographical form. As a result "perception" as such is both a thematic issue—centering on the hero's experience—and a narrative strategy. And the crucial importance of perception, as both moral experience and narrative technique, is emphasized by the opening sentence of the novel: "But Dante's hell is heaven. Look at things in another light. Not always the smarting blue glare pressing through the glass. Another light, or darkness. Wherever we'd go to rest. By the simple rivers of our time" (p. 9).

The statement is both a criticism of certain forms of perception and a demonstration, by way of the narrative language itself, of more acceptable perspectives. Baraka's narrator is inviting us to discard rigidly rationalistic and excessively abstract values that are symbolized by the blue (-eyed) "glare" of white Western culture. These values are also inherent in the rationalistic preference for detached observation (looking at things through a glass). But from Baraka's viewpoint this kind of perception is inadequate because narrow and rigid perspectives cannot cope with the complexities of experience and time—with the "rivers" of time. In other words, the continuing flow of time-as-experience can only be apprehended in its entirety by that kind of perspective which itself duplicates the flow of experience and which, in turn, is duplicated by the free flow of "sounds" and visual "images" in Baraka's narrative style.

In the immediate context of Baraka's statement, for example, the exhortation to look at "things" implies two sets of meanings. On one level it attacks the treatment of people as things, especially the neutrals of the Vestibule; and as we have already seen, this attack is directed at the moral and social traditions represented by Dante's Western culture. And, on a second level, "things" connotes life or experience as a whole—the kind of total experience that the novel proposes to explore. In effect, Baraka's explanation of his narrative purpose (the exploration of things-as-experience) exemplifies the technique of his novel. By associating the image of things-as-neutrals with the concept of things-as-experience, the author compels his reader to perceive both ideas at once. And in the process Baraka allows the reader to comprehend, simultaneously, both the *immedi-ate* object of the Vestibule episode (the neutrals) and the *subsequent* experiences to be dramatized by the narrative as a whole.

"Things" is therefore an associationist image, as Baraka himself uses the term in his own epilogue to the novel. It links two narrative contexts (in this instance, present and future); it juxtaposes the analysis of one specific experience (neutrality) with the exploration of experience as a whole; and in the process it allows the novelist to present past, present, and future in a single moment of simultaneously perceived events. This kind of associationist technique also provides Baraka with the kind of narrative viewpoint which is ideally suited to his autobiographical form. In Baraka's associationist handling of his hero's autobiography, Roi's development, and his description of that growth, are not based on a simple movement from one point to another, like the line on a graph. In pondering and describing his experiences Roi is simultaneously conscious of both his past and his present, and he is also aware that his future will be molded by his present in much the same way that the past has influenced his present. In his own words, "I am and was and will be . . ." (p. 153).

So that while the reader can trace the narrator's development on a linear or sequential pattern based on clock-time (ghetto boyhood to mainstream adulthood), the narrator's autobiographical consciousness—his narrative viewpoint—is constantly *associating* past with present, anticipating the future, and fusing all of these into single moments of complex awareness. And this kind of fusion, or juxtaposition, of events and experiences is the primary effect of Baraka's associationist images. Thus from as early as the first circle of Roi's hell, the heathen's self-loathing, as liar, can also be read as the hero's autobiographical reflections, in the "present," on what he has been in the "past" (p. 13).

This juxtaposition of present self-knowledge and former self-deception is even more explicit when the narrator forces the reader to participate in his experience. The act of reading Roi's self-description in the present compels the reader to experience Roi's past. In the narrator's words, "This thing, if you read it, will jam your face in my shit" (p. 15). And finally, this moment of self-loathing as a lying heathen anticipates, and is eventually recalled by, Roi's subsequent confession to Peaches that he has lived the life of a liar (p. 140). Here, in brief, we have a revealing example of the manner in which the protagonist's narrative (autobiographical) viewpoint integrates different moments of experience within the narrative design: he associates distinct episodes, times, and judgments and describes them accordingly. And in turn the whole is linked with the reader's own sensibilities in that the reader too is persuaded that his or her consciousness simultaneously grasps a variety of "things." On this basis, the merging of narrative technique and themes is all but complete. And this is the kind of accomplishment that makes *Dante's Hell* one of Baraka's most impressive works.

CHAPTER 4

The Short Stories

I *Major Themes of* Tales

BARAKA'S major short stories appear in the collection *Tales,*
which was published in 1967. They were originally published in
literary magazines in the early and middle 1960s, and it is therefore
safe to assume that for the most part they represent Baraka's early
work in the genre. The usual signs of that early phase of his development are clear enough. There is the rigorous emphasis on the integration of form and content, so that the two become one and indivisible,
as they are in *Dante's Hell,* rather than functioning merely as vehicles
for each other. And here too narrative style relies heavily on "associationist" images of sounds and sight which are themselves the thematic
experience rather than merely illustrations of that experience.
Moreover these two features of the short stories complement each
other as they do in Baraka's novel. And this similarity is appropriate
since the stories resume one of the dominant themes of the novel: hell
has been redefined in terms of social milieu (black America) and
psychological experience (the crisis generated by black self-hatred or
"imitation" whiteness).

"A Chase" advertises the link with the novel, and with Dante's
Inferno by way of its subtitle ("Alighieri's Dream"). The story as a
whole is a nightmarish series of images through which the writer
presents an overview of life in the black ghetto. "Uncle Tom's Cabin:
Alternate Ending" probes the puritanism and the limited intellectualism which Baraka sees as the (white) alternative to the black
ghetto. And in "The Death of Horatio Alger" a certain ethnic naiveté
about black life in white America is beginning to give way to another,
more realistic, awareness. Here, as in *Dante's Hell,* the death or
ending signifies new beginnings, albeit of a tentative kind.

The grouping of the stories is not necessarily chronological. Instead
they are thematically defined. Hence there are two sets of stories that

84

center on the private self. In one group the black experience in white America damages the individual sensibility, and in this context hell appears as the symbol of that feeling of isolation which results from psychic damage. In the other group isolation is not simply the result of a fragmenting social environment. It is, instead, the creative though lonely experience of self-exploration—a positive kind of aloneness. In this regard "The Death of Horatio Alger" witnesses the death of one kind of isolation—that resulting from racial naiveté—and the birth-pangs of another. Moreover, self-exploratory aloneness is not an exclusively racial experience in these stories. In its most complex sense it results from a variety of perceptions and experiences, each centered on the nature of the imagination: the protagonist's experience demonstrates the limits and strengths of the imagination as a means of self-discovery and self-analysis in a world that does not seem to encourage the acceptance of subjective modes like the imagination.

The doubts surrounding the effectiveness of the imagination link the stories of self-exploration with yet another group, with those stories which concentrate on the artist, particularly the writer, and on the artist's view of his role in society. Like the imagination itself the artist is invested with an ambiguous identity (insightful but limited, even impotent at times)—especially in "Going Down Slow," "Heroes Are Gang Leaders," "Salute," "Words," and "New-Sense." The limitations of the writer are partly the result of society's indifference to things of the spirit and the imagination. But as Baraka's growing black nationalism increasingly defines his short-story themes in the middle 1960s there is a corresponding shift in the implications of the writer's sense of impotence. As we have already noted in his political essays, the urgent need for action, especially action that brings about substantive social change, fosters a certain skepticism in Baraka about the effectiveness of the writer's tools—words. Words are therefore suspect in stories like "Salute" and "Words," not only because they are in themselves an inadequate substitute for effective activism, but also because the *literary* words are culturally suspect. Consequently, even in the hands of the black nationalist writer the literary word is an emblem of a certain indebtedness to the white, Western culture against which the literary word is being directed.

Tales, like other works from the same period, displays Baraka's characteristic ambivalence in the early and middle years of his writing toward his Western literary background. On the one hand the writer cherishes the literary word as iconic image, as the very essence of the experience that it describes. But on the other hand the political activist rebels against the reflective, analytical function of the written word in Western culture ("New-Sense"), even as he expresses serious doubts about the overall effectiveness of the word in any form. Baraka's black nationalism does offer a solution in that some of the stories in the collection attempt to turn away from standard literary English to the oral nuances of black urban idioms. Hence the collective title, *Tales*, connotes an orality that is not normally associated with the short story as literary form in Western literature. Or, in the case of "The Screamers," Baraka turns to the nonverbal modes of jazz in the black musical tradition.

On balance the results are quite similar to Baraka's weighing of the relative merits of black music and black literature in his essays: the oral traditions and the musical forms of black folk culture—the black "roots"—are asserted to be superior to the black writer, to his literary words and to those sensibilities which he borrowed from the West together with those words. As in *Dante's Hell* the writer emerges from all of this as a deeply divided, intensely ambiguous self. His sense of paralysis is symptomatic of the condition of all blacks like himself—educated, well read, and therefore separated (in Baraka's view) from black American culture by a "white" intellectuality. But the very process of exploring that paralysis is an act of release: it frees him to be candid about his divided identity; and paradoxically enough that candor effects a certain freedom, however limited at first, from intellectual bondage to the West—in much the same way that, on the other side of the coin, a certain indebtedness to the West is confirmed by the very intensity with which the West is being rejected.

"The Death of Horatio Alger" is a bridge of sorts between those stories which continue the themes of *Dante's Hell* by exploring black life in America-as-hell and those works which announce a growing black nationalism. In "The Screamers" a jam session at a jazz nightclub sparks racial anger at white society and inspires a communal celebration of black ethnicity. And these black nationalist themes are particularly explicit and urgent in the final four stories of the collection, "New Spirit," "No Body No Place," "Now and Then," and "Answers in Progress." Given the increasing bent toward black nationalism it is not surprising that the largest group of stories are black nationalist in theme and tone. At the same time there is an increasingly urgent need on the writer's part to transform his art into some kind of committed action.

On the whole, then, *Tales* represents a variety of moods and goals, together with corresponding narrative techniques. This very variety reflects Baraka's mind at a crucial point in his career. The inherited forms of the literary word are obviously still exerting a powerful influence. But they are also counterbalanced by the growing pressures of his political activism and by those nonverbal folk traditions which black cultural nationalism makes particularly attractive. The exploration of the private self brings with it a heightened self-consciousness that is almost sensuous in its intensity in "The Largest Ocean in the World." But the pleasures of self-exploration may also be seductive, escapist, and consequently they need to be counterbalanced by the group conscience of ethnic commitment. On the one hand, there is a growing sense of political urgency, particularly on the need for effective, substantive action. And, on the other hand, there is the persistent awareness that art and the experience which art reenacts are composed of a multiplicity of levels, with correspondingly multiple choices. This sense of multiplicity arises, ironically enough, from the very fact that this is a transitional stage in Baraka's career; and it also accounts for the fact that *Tales*, like *Dante's Hell*, represents his consistently best work.

II *Hell as Theme and Image*

Tales is generally less allusive than *Dante's Hell*. The reader of the short stories will not encounter the host of names which, in the novel, attest to Baraka's formidable reading. But it is significant that some of the more explicit references to Western literature occur in stories that continue the main theme of the novel—the hellish experience of being black in a white world and of being "unfocused" on one's racial identity. The idea of hell is invested with a special irony in "Uncle Tom's Cabin: Alternate Ending." The story is really an exposé of white puritanism as a kind of hell that enmeshes America's archetypal liberators—those white liberals who are heirs to the New England humanitarianism of Harriet Beecher Stowe, author of the original *Uncle Tom's Cabin*. The narrative format is fairly conventional here, depending far less on associationist images than do most of the other stories. The choice of format is significant. As in the novel, the "straight" narrative structure is associated with a narrow rationalism and with a schematic morality that fosters Dantesque images of hell ("The ones we Westerners like to make art out of").

The embodiment of what Baraka sees as the real hell is a white woman. She is Miss Orbach, the fifth-grade teacher at a school where

Eddie McGhee is one of her black pupils. Miss Orbach is a package of inhibitions—the sexual restraint which confuses "purity" and "superiority," the class consciousness which establishes permanent barriers between herself and the "thriving children of the thriving lower middle classes" (p. 16),[1] and the submerged racial animosity which, having been consciously denied for the sake of liberalism, can now only take the form of a vague uneasiness with her black charges. The racial uneasiness becomes overt hostility when one of those charges, Eddie McGhee, clearly demonstrates that he is not the helpless darky of the Uncle Tom tradition, by correctly answering questions in class and by showing signs of a marked independence of Miss Orbach herself. In effect the absence of an Uncle Tom deprives the white liberal teacher of her *raison d'etre*.

Miss Orbach retaliates by reporting to the school doctor that Eddie might be suffering from a serious disease which might account for his "unusual" demeanor in class. Eddie reports this to his parents and the following morning Miss Orbach is summoned to a conference between Eddie's mother and the school principal. Upon entering the principal's office Miss Orbach's eyes meet Mrs. McGhee's, and the teacher promptly falls in love with the mother. The story ends at this point. On the basis of plot and theme this is probably the weakest story of the collection. Miss Orbach's character is too underdeveloped to sustain the kind of attitudes which Baraka wishes to attribute to her as individual and social archetype. And the other personalities are equally lacking in the kind of persuasive complexity which the theme seems to demand of them.

What does salvage the story is the incisive satire which reverses traditional values and roles. Miss Orbach is heiress to the puritan morality of white America and to the abstractionism of the West. Moreover these two traditions merge in the white liberalism which she represents and which Baraka now traces to Harriet Beecher Stowe. But it is the white liberal rather than the black who is now the slave—to puritanism, to a repressed racism, and to a cold-blooded rationalism. And her liberation which depends upon absolute integrity about her sexuality rests on blacks, on their acceptance of her sexual needs and her humanity as a whole. In attacking the archetypal roles fostered by *Uncle Tom's Cabin* Baraka criticizes white liberalism as a condescending protectiveness, as the psychic enslavement of white liberals and their black victims alike. The shock effect of that lesbian taboo upon which the story ends dramatizes the radical reversal of roles. The reversal rests on the need to break away from certain moral conventions and from certain racial stereotypes.

In "A Chase (Alighieri's Dream)" the allusion to Dante's *Inferno* sets the stage for a plot which is not "straight" narrative but a series of images. But these images are woven into a certain continuity by the very idea of a dream. More specifically, the original dream-vision which is the basis of Dante's narrative in *The Inferno* has been adopted to become Baraka's nightmare of the ghetto streets. And this recurrent street image, together with the nightmarish quality of the images altogether, provides "A Chase" with its narrative cohesion.

The street leads from the broken plans in the rural black South to urban "cages of decay" in the North, to their cemeteries and their Saturday "beer smells." The smells of decay are complemented by a pervasive sense of death, ranging from the collapse of those dreams which inspired the move from the South, to the sexual impotence ("dead cocks") that suggests the psychic death of the North's victims. The dream-turned-nightmare is symbolized by the street image of search, movement, quest. Moreover, the street as a generally urban symbol emphasizes that this is not only a black American dream. As in Ann Petry's first-rate novel, *The Street* (1946), it is the all-American dream, or myth, of social equality, justice for all, and unlimited rewards for unlimited individual effort. The death of the dream is therefore fraught with implications for all Americans. Hence, for example, the dead faces of blacks are slowly ground into dust in the street that runs beside the cemeteries of "crooked old jews." The anti-Semitic reference joins the images of the black dead to confirm the poisonous social effects of the failure of the dream: the disillusioned blacks now perceive their traditional "fellow-sufferers" (Jews) as part of the exploitive white structure, and at the same time their response partakes of the anti-Semitic attitudes of the very society which they resent.

The tragedy of the dream lies not only in its failure, but also in its very essence (as a lie from beginning to end). Thus the ubiquitous street symbol emphasizes the hellish (and therefore nightmarish) qualities of the dream by presenting it as a futile quest. At best it leads, in the event of "successful" achievement, away from one's humanity, "straight at the moon." Considered either as a symbol of the dream's falsity or as an emblem of its hollow successes, the moon-goal of the dream-street is associated with sterility—the emotional sterility that is represented by the virginal moon goddess ("Diane") and by her lover's inert ("dead") penis.

But the street is not only a thoroughfare of death. It is also a life-style. It is a rough life-style with death always lurking in the background; but, as in *Dante's Hell*, the ghetto street is a vital setting—for a boys' basketball game, for example, or for a visit to the neighborhood milk bar. The hip fake of the basketball game is therefore more than a bit of slick playground expertise. It is symptomatic of *being* hip, of knowing one's environment and whatever else one needs for survival. To be hip in this sense is to be street-wise. But this hipness is not limited to street-wisdom, since the latter is valuable only in so far as one elects, or is forced, to accept *everything* that the street represents as the sum total of one's existence. A more profound and far-reaching hipness, the one with which the story concludes, recognizes that the street is a universal condition with the "entire world" visible from its corners.

But this recognition implies more than simply accepting that condition as the basis for life, or more precisely, for survival. It is also the recognition that leads to eventual change. The view of the entire world is one that goes "even to the lower regions." And the allusion to the lower regions of Dante's dream-inferno represents not only Baraka's alienation from Dante's literary heritage but also a certain hostility to the entire culture that enshrines the heritage. This is the kind of alienation or hostility that heralds possible change, and as such it is an integral part of that hipness which perceives the black American condition both in its distinctiveness and in its universal implications.

"The Alternative" is a more extensive but less successful attempt to use images as short-story narrative. As the title suggests Baraka is presenting here the alternative to the ghetto street—middle-class affluence and respectability by way of a college education and cultural assimilation. The setting is a university residence. The images and the brief narrative vignettes coalesce to form impressions of middle-class vulgarity, moral emptiness, and intellectual sterility. As Roi discovers in *Dante's Hell*, the middle-class alternative (represented here by university life) is another hell. The story is the most allusive of the collection. There are allusions to Rousseau, Thomas Hobbes, Albert Camus, and Yeats ("The Second Coming") among others.

The allusions are more important as symptoms of a certain intellectual milieu than as specific statements. This is the intellectual milieu of the middle class. And the academic images of literary and philosophical traditions are combined with other images (Brooks Brothers references, for example) to emphasize the middle-class direction to which a college education leads. This direction is presented within the kind of subjective context that dominates the themes of *Dante's Hell*. In this story the subjective experience on which the narrative form is based is centered on the personality of Ray McGhee. He is the leader of his group of college friends, by virtue of his erudition, his mastery of academe's intellectual tools and values.

He is also a study in alienation in a sterile, destructive sense. The erudition that is the key to middle-class success and future leadership also sets him apart from other blacks, even from those who, like himself, have chosen the middle-class "alternative," but who have been less assimilated into white culture precisely because they are less "erudite." Ray's isolation is therefore a kind of moral bankruptcy. As the "leader" he sits at the center of the story—that is, at the center of his peers' obsessive attention. But from another point of view he is perpetually on the sidelines, without "cause or place. Except talk, feeling guilt" (p. 18). When one of the students knocks him to the floor in a brief scuffle the violence confirms Ray's isolation, an isolation that is further intensified by the concluding image of the story: Ray, lying alone on a floor that reeks of age and Protestantism, tries to compensate for his isolation from other black students with the assumption that he has been accepted by that other world which is represented by the Protestant floor (p. 29).

On the whole, "The Alternative" bears the marks of that imaginative energy which works so well in "A Chase." The narrative images are effective in that they do reveal Ray's subjective world—the private torture of his divided ethnic consciousness—as well as the telltale vulgarity of the world around him. But on balance "The Alternative" is less well written. It suffers from a certain overabundance. The portrayal of students and their middle-class vulgarity is unconvincing because it lacks control. The profusion of images results in a numbing sense of hyperbole rather than a convincing narration. In a curiously perverse way the abundance of images becomes monotonous after a while. They are victims of their own excess, the kind of excess which almost invariably plagues Baraka's writing whenever he tries to exorcize the (white) middle-class demon from the black American's cultural spirit.

III *Alienation and Isolation*

Ray McGhee's is only one of several examples of racial alienation in *Tales*. "The Death of Horatio Alger" also explores the isolating effect of racial self-hatred, but proceeds beyond this to imply the beginnings of a positive ethnic awareness. In terms of myth the death of the all-American success archetype (Horatio Alger) is purely symbolic and represents the death of naive illusions about America itself in the mind of a young black boy. And this symbolic death signalizes a less accepting, more ethnically aware view. The young boy is Mickey, and significantly the setting of the symbolic death within him is "the dozens"—a black American word game of insults directed at the participants' parents.

As the story opens Mickey and his closest friend, J.D., are playing "the dozens." J.D. loses his temper very quickly (and therefore loses the game) when three white boys who misunderstand the game take the insults literally and laugh at the exchanges. In his anger J.D. strikes Mickey and then they both beat up the white boys. Mickey is completely humiliated by the incident, partly because J.D. attacks him in the presence of their friends, and partly because the whites' shallow response to the game jolts his own complacency about white America and its myths—especially Horatio Alger myths about equality and freedom. His rage at the white world inspires a new love (an intense sense of brotherhood) for J.D. But this love is counterbalanced by the humiliation that he feels. Thus he proceeds to yell insults at J.D. in a serious and potentially deadly variation on "the dozens." This is no longer a game but a kind of violence in which blacks like Mickey and J.D. abuse each other out of frustration with the world around them. J.D. is a better fighter, and he whips Mickey until the latter's parents intervene.

But the violent note on which the story ends is not altogether negative. The hatred which Mickey directs at J.D. is really an exorcism of his own racial self-hatred—the kind of self-hatred that is implicit in having previously loved white symbols (freckles, sandy hair, the flag) as the shaping images in his life. The fight with J.D. is therefore a kind of self-cleansing. It is also inspired by the frustration of being unable to communicate his emerging sense of brotherhood with J.D. Hence, by a similar token, the note of isolation which is felt at the end of the story is partly positive. In stripping himself of insensitive white friends and Horatio Alger images of American society, Mickey is putting an end to his alienation from his black identity. At the same time there is no guarantee that he will fully realize that more creative sense of ethnic self toward which he is now painfully reaching. Hence the feeling of isolation persists. But insofar as this isolation results from the death of his old Horatio Alger psyche and the end of his previous alienation from blackness, then it connotes a creative process.

On the whole, then, isolation is an ambiguous experience in "The Death of Horatio Alger." At its worst it is a self-destructive alienation from self and race; but at best it is a transitional phase in the movement toward racial awareness. Like Roi in *Dante's Hell* Mickey's feelings of isolation force him to confront the "heresy" of racial self-hatred. And throughout all of this Baraka seems to imply a distinction between isolation as aloneness and the condition that results from the willful, or culturally conditioned, act of alienating oneself from one's racial experience. "The Largest Ocean in the World" offers further insights into this kind of distinction. The title itself evokes an overwhelming sense of aloneness. This aloneness dominates the brief story, based on a series of images that pass through the protagonist's mind as he walks along a deserted street. These images vary, from concrete impressions of his surroundings to fantasies. And at all times Baraka counterbalances the imaginative or subjective perception of the environment with the manner in which the imagination turns inwardly upon itself from time to time. It is this propensity to turn inward, to shut out the outside world, that makes Baraka suspicious of the isolated imagination: "There are men who live in themselves so they think their minds will create a different place of ecstasy" (p. 32).

On the whole, then, Baraka makes an important distinction here between the imagination as a key to subjective truths and that kind of self-loving imagination which permits the protagonist to see no one and to want no one. This is the kind of self-love that afflicts Ray McGhee in "The Alternative." It is a disease that Baraka attributes to the white world, where narrow cultural traditions allegedly foster habits of self-contained imaginativeness just as much as they encourage the exclusive reliance on reason for its own sake. Hence the "imitation" whites of "The Alternative" and *Dante's Hell* actually demonstrate their immersion in white culture by their self-indulgent habits of isolation—either as excessively rationalistic types or as inward-looking, isolated imaginations. But, paradoxically, in all of these works the very process of indicating the danger of a self-centered imagination also has the effect of emphasizing the creative power of the imagination as a subjective mode which, in a healthy context of social awareness, can lead to a complex, creative consciousness of both self and society.

The man walking the streets in "The Largest Ocean" therefore goes through distinct phases of perception, each reflecting Baraka's interest in the relationship between the imagination and subjective experience. And this movement in perception, coinciding with the central image of the walker, defines the narrative structure of this finely executed story. First there are simply a series of fairly "concrete" images of the sights and sounds of the street (dark corners, cold stones, voices of students, and so forth). These are basically unreflective images, but they are followed by a more introspective mood in which he shuts out the outside world, in which he wants no one. His "hundred thoughts" about himself are thoughts of sickness, death, and a longing to suck in the darkness around him—a longing to die.

Then, having demonstrated the self-destructive potential of a wholly isolated imagination, Baraka takes his protagonist into the third and final stage, one in which self-indulgent fantasies give way to an imaginative exploration of self in relation to the environment. The protagonist explores himself with his hands, feeling himself sway gently as he strides: "He is a soft young girl, running his hands over his own body" (p. 34). This androgynous image is particularly effective because it succeeds an earlier image of the protagonist kissing himself. His imaginative experience has shifted from self-love as extreme isolation and self-indulgence (the kiss) to that exploration of self and body which allows him to imagine himself in the complex, rather than selfishly simplified, dimensions suggested by the androgynous image. In other words, the growing capacity to perceive himself not merely as one (and a totally isolated one at that) but as two-in-one (male-and-female) signals the ability to link his self-perception with an awareness of another self: imagination as limited self-love is being transformed into a creative subjectivity which integrates self with others. And at the very moment of this crucial transformation, he is ready to see others and to rejoin the world around him: he waves at a passing car (p. 34).

IV   *The Writer as Divided Self*

The ambivalence with which Baraka views the imagination in *Tales* has a direct bearing on his handling of the writer's personality in these stories. As we have already seen, the crucial role of the imagination as subjective experience is linked in Baraka's work with the value which he places on the subjective, as opposed to the narrowly "objective." The frequency with which he returns to the figure of the writer attests to this special interest in the role of the imagination. Quite apart from stories like "The Alternative" in which the protagonist almost invariably has some interest in literature, there are several others in which the protagonists are writers—"Going Down," "Heroes," "Salute," "Words," "New-Sense," and "Unfinished." The isolation in which these writer-protagonists live underscores the special aloneness of the writer in a world which is hostile to the imagination, particularly the artistic imagination. And this peculiar, isolated role is the logical extension of Baraka's continuing distinction between art as a frequently self-contained form, and art as an ideally committed and activist kind of subjectivity.

But the distinctiveness of art, even the committed kind, often implies some kind of separation from society; and when the writer elects to be insulated from society that distinctiveness amounts to what Baraka regards as an unhealthy aesthetic—"art for art's sake"— that is simply an extension of the self-indulgent imagination. And since this unhealthy aesthetic is associated with white culture, then its presence in the black writer is a symptom of racial self-hatred: in such cases the intrinsic escapism of the self-indulgent imagination is linked with racial or cultural escape.

Lew Crosby's "escape" in "Going Down Slow" takes the form of drugs and sex rather than racial self-hatred as such. He sleeps with Leah Powell and is the last to discover that his wife, Racheal, sleeps with Mauro. His philandering is a symptom of Lew's inability to deal with people. Leah is therefore a bedtime escape rather than someone with whom he can really be involved. He is a "neo-shithead, a neo-dope" whose inability to deal with reality takes the form of escapist fantasies: "Fantasies replaced each other. Fantasies replaced realities. Realities did not replace anything" (p. 53). In fact even his self-conscious emphasis on his identity as a writer becomes an extension of that deep-seated need to escape: he wishes to write about himself without being involved with others (p. 55). And it is typical of his inveterate escapism that he flees Mauro's apartment, after striking his rival down, without pausing to find out if he has killed him.

Because Lew's perceptions also function as the sole narrative viewpoint in the story then the reader is forced to participate in Lew's characteristic need to escape from reality. We remain as ignorant of the outcome of Lew's actions as he himself chooses to be. Instead we join him, after the attack on Mauro, at a friend's apartment, where he indulges in another form of escape—getting high on drugs "just out of everybody's reach" (p. 61). Indeed, the story owes much of its effectiveness to that frankly subjective narrative format which immerses Baraka's reader in Lew's escapism, and in effect transforms the story itself into an extended example of Lew's escapist habits.

This narrative tactic is also applied to "Heroes Are Gang Leaders." It is equally effective here despite differences between the stories. "Going Down Slow" is a fast-moving narrative with the pace reflecting Lew's frenetic attempts to escape. "Heroes" is slower, and the pace befits the setting, a hospital room that the writer-protagonist shares with a derelict who is being questioned by police about an attempted suicide. But the slower pace here is also due to the more deliberately reflective self-searching of the protagonist; and the narrative details consist primarily of a series of self-scrutinizing images. These images are ambiguous. Like Lew Crosby this writer is an escapist who frankly admits that his concerns are not centered on people. But this protagonist is more ruthlessly candid about his escapism and its destructive effects on his art: words, he admits, are "useless unless people can carry them" (p. 63); and despite the potential usefulness of the literary word people like himself have simply become hedonists (p. 65).

On the whole this train of reflection creates the impression of a mind coming to grips with reality in the very process of attempting to analyze the limitations of the escapist imagination. But the ultimate irony of the story rests in the fact that even this candid self-portrait amounts to a kind of evasion in the long run, because when the writer does have an opportunity to become involved in a truly committed way he shies away. His train of thought is literally interrupted by physical reality. The police are bullying the derelict who is unable to talk because the acid with which he attempted suicide destroyed his vocal cords. The protagonist intercedes briefly and points out that the man has lost his voice. The police rebuff him and he immediately retreats to his books in order to "rub out their image" (p.69). The real world with its demands for commitment interrupts only momentarily those reflections which are themselves a form of escape, despite the degree to which they critically examine the implications of escapism.

There is a crucial link between the writer's reading of literature (his literary heritage) and his views of his own art in "Heroes." The escapism that is attributed to that literary heritage ("some rich lady's candy") becomes the source of the protagonist's failure to be truly committed (p. 68). Baraka expands upon this theme in "Salute." Here the protagonist is not specifically identified as a writer, but he is clearly presented as someone in the process of clarifying his intellectual directions. He is serving in the air force, and both the military career and his voracious reading in Western literature represent, as they do in *Dante's Hell*, an unhealthy escape into an alien, destructive culture. As a result he suffers from the familiar paralysis and isolation of the escapist. Thus he really has nothing to say when he is reprimanded by a white officer for failing to salute—at least nothing that actually responds to the racial motives behind the officer's insistence on military etiquette: "But I said something, you know, the kind of shit you'd say, you know" (p. 87). The lameness of that concluding remark has a telling effect. The protagonist's verbal limpness, both to the officer and to the reader, is a symptom of his intellectual and moral limitations. And that pointed comparison with the reader broadens the scope of the narrative from guilty self-scrutiny to a satiric dig at intellectuals everywhere.

The very brief "Words" could, for all practical purposes, be a sequel to "Salute." Here the writer is completely out of place in a Harlem bar. He is caught up in the "objective stance" and "alien language of another tribe." Here too the intellectual's acquired habits of rational objectivity create distance between himself and others, at the same time that his self-centered imagination cuts him off from his environment. As a result his words, in art and in conversation, remain merely words. His saving grace, as in the case of the writer in "Heroes," is that he recognizes his limitations: he knows that he needs to exploit his isolation as an opportunity for that kind of healthy self-exploration which will end his crippling alienation from people: "We can be quiet and think and love the silence. We need to look at trees more closely. We need to listen" (p. 91).

While "love" is a self-centered retreat into silence in "Words," it represents the ideal of involvement and commitment in "New-Sense," where it is contrasted with the self-loving withdrawal that Baraka exposes in the other stories. In the first section of "New-Sense," "love" is synonymous with sex, a mechanical and emotionally empty kind of sexual encounter between the black protagonist and a white woman. The interracial interlude is an allegory of the black writer's lifelong involvement with Western intellectual standards (logic and "objectivity") which have isolated him from the realities of being black in a white culture. Consequently his artistic imagination is really an extension of that isolation.

In turn as he confronts the "ugly reality" of his isolation the writer yearns for a different experience in which he makes love, for example, instead of just hacking away at a machine (p. 95). The machine reference obviously continues the emphasis on the mechanical nature of loveless sex and uninvolved art: it combines the image of mechanical sex with the symbol of the writer's machine (the typewriter). In yearning for love he is therefore reaching for Baraka's familiar ideal of wholeness in which experience remains integrated (the physical, the emotional and intellectual) rather than separate.

And this capacity to yearn for a sense of wholeness signalizes a shift from a divided self. The shift is significant, not only for the writer himself, but for all blacks who are "caught up" in Western values to the point where they are alienated from their ethnic identity. He symbolizes those blacks to whom he feels drawn by ethnic love and artistic commitment. But he still remains distinct by virtue of his art. The artist's self-destructive alienation is being replaced by a sense of commitment that still leaves room for the recognition of his distinctive role as artist.

Of course, this is a continuing process. Its incompleteness is clearly enunciated in the title and theme of "Unfinished." The impressionistic images upon which the narrative depends are drawn from a summer night in Harlem. Despite a rather rambling style, the story does dramatize the writer's growing sense of commitment to the black community. But this is rendered with a sense of incompleteness that provides a crucial air of realism, and consequently the new ethnic loyalties must coexist awkwardly with the old allegiances to the mentors (Herman Melville) from another culture. And the black world to which the newly committed writer reaches with so much love does not always prove itself to be entirely lovable. It is a world of talk, love and blood; but blood connotes violence as well as blood brotherhood, love is often counterbalanced by self-hatred, and talk, as usual in Baraka's work, can be escape from action as well as necessary communication. Here, too, the writer remains a symbol of the black experience at large; for even his own incomplete sense of becoming is a symptom of the unfinished nature of black consciousness in his world.

V   Toward Black Nationalism

This impression of incompleteness is, of course, also attributable to the essentially divided self of the writer who, however ethnically committed to black America, operates in a medium that symptomizes a certain indebtedness to the West. In *Tales*, as in his essays, Baraka turns to the black musician as artist-archetype whenever he needs a symbol of an unambiguous black consciousness. He does this in "The Screamers," a story set in a Newark jazz club. The narrative centers on the patrons' responses on separate nights to jamming sessions by saxophonists Big Jay and Lynn Hope. Having been whipped up to a frenzy by Big Jay's performance, the crowd then challenges Lynn Hope, by its very presence, to outdo Big Jay. Lynn Hope accepts the challenge. He not only captivates the crowd inside the club, but mesmerizes them into marching behind him into the streets outside, with their own screams both responding to and inciting the screams of the saxophone. The marchers are quickly joined by people on the streets—and traffic jams, a riot, and violent police action follow in rapid succession.

There is no attempt to glamorize these events. The "conked" hair of some patrons is a familiar symbol of racial self-hatred; the pervasive violence of the environment is emphasized by brutally casual references to former patrons who had been beaten and left for dead outside; and the narrator and his friends are like predators on the prowl for "meat" (women) as they seek out partners for the evening. Moreover the music has its explosive impact precisely because it expresses so accurately the frustrations and violence of the cultural experience out of which it has arisen. Big Jay's horn therefore spits "enraged sociologies" (p. 77). And Lynn Hope's riffs are not simply musical notes in some aesthetically "pure" sense. They are screams expressing the musician's "evaluation of the world" (p. 78).

But even in the act of reflecting despair and pain the music and its audience represent an affirmative process. The music expresses an ethnic and social idealism, a "clear image of ourselves as we should always be," a committed sense of artistic form as committed statement ("the form of the sweetest revolution"), and the audience's growing sense of community (p. 79). Music as a grass-roots form therefore achieves what the inherited literary word seems incapable of doing decisively in *Tales*: it creates, however fleetingly, a complete sense of individual ethnicity and communal spirit. And on an aesthetic level music, when perceived in such terms, is most compatible with Baraka's ideal of form and image as meaning. Lynn Hope's riffs and Big Jay's improvisations are tonal images that are in their very essence the summary of social "meanings" (experience). The "scream" of the instrument is simultaneously, and indistinguishably, musical and sociological; the screams of the audience are integrated with the music (in the African, and Afro-American traditions of statement and audience response); and at the same time the screams of both audience and musician coalesce to voice a powerful feeling of community.

At this point the very idea of completeness and wholeness is intrinsic to the performance—to the nature of the music itself, to its relationship with the audience, and to the audience's response. And this all has the effect of bestowing some kind of legitimacy on the short story as literary form—by virtue of the writer's ability in this instance to infuse his literary narration with the symbols and insights of the musical "narration" (performance). In this regard Baraka is clearly emphasizing, as he does in his essays, that the writer's art can only approximate a sense of ethnic or cultural wholeness when it is integrated with aspects of black nonliterary forms. But for all that, the very use of the short-story format has a special significance in a work like "The Screamers." The story, in the final analysis, does not present some unconditional victory of blackness over self-hatred or white power. Despite the untrammeled significance of the music as experience and notwithstanding the sense of wholeness with which the audience shares that experience, the moment of completeness is as transitory as the feelings of power which lead the audience into a street riot. Consequently the short story's cultural background as a borrowed Western form allows Baraka to remind the reader of the persistent Western modes and the intransigent facts of white power which eventually reassert themselves after brief moments of ethnic completeness in a small part of the black community.

Unlike the stories centered wholly on the writer's personality, "The Screamers" celebrates the actual achievement of a certain level of ethnic consciousness. Whatever sense of limitations one feels in the work arises largely from an awareness that the maintenance and spreading of that consciousness has hardly begun. It must still overcome black self-destructiveness as well as white antipathy, and for these reasons is still largely futuristic as a dominant social force. This blend of present limitations and future possibilities shapes the theme of black nationalism in the final stories of the collection.

"New Spirit" is an elegaic work set in a funeral parlor where the protagonist pays last respects to his dead lover, Bumi. As he looks on the corpse he reflects on the lovelessness and deadliness of that Christian world that is represented by the ritualistic trappings of the funeral. And that world is contrasted with the love of self and others which the relationship with Bumi has represented. The narrative is disjointed and rambling, but in an effective way. As the narrator admits in his concluding statement, all of this does not make clear-cut sense: experience itself seems disjointed when lovelessness and hatred persist, while relationships based on love are terminated by death. The narrative form therefore reflects both this sense of disjointed reality and the narrator's incoherent reflections on it all.

The ideal of love also informs the theme of "No Body No Place." Here the communal and ethnic significance of love is more explicit in what is not so much a narrative as it is a series of reflections on the nature of love as a creative, collective experience. The demand to love and be loved is a demand to be alive, to be beautiful, and to be accepted as human. Love as a social ideal in action should link individuals, knit the community, and (by virtue of its creative possibilities) represent the very idea of a godhead. At this point god is not even the ambiguous deity of *Dante's Hell*, where the divine image is both white Christian and black. Here the idea of the godhead is emphatically subjective: it is the individual's sense of perfectibility within a human community that is perceived as perfectible.

"No Body No Place" is therefore a vision of future possibilities rather than a "realistic" impression of things as they are. It envisages "future evolutions" as these are projected through the narrator's imagination. And on this basis the subjectivity of the writer's artistic imagination and the subjective vision of the political idealist become one. In other words, content (political commitment) and form (narrative technique) are indivisible in this story, thereby exemplifying that integration of activism and art which underlies the general excellence of the *Tales* collection.

"Now and Then," as the title indicates, dramatizes the continuing tensions between the traditional attitudes and the ethnic possibilities that are so clearly articulated in "The Screamers" (pp. 117–25). These tensions are reflected in the contrasts that the story evokes between the language of standard American English and black American idiom, between "now," replete with emerging ethnic values, and "then," with its dominant self-hatred. The narrative itself is really a report on what is being said in the black community, and it consequently represents the variety of viewpoints that constitute the thematic and stylistic tensions of the story as a whole. The description of musicians, for example, is couched in standard English: "The music would climb, and bombard everything" (p. 117). But beyond the writer's own literary word the story concludes with the ritualistic religious chant ("MMMMMMMMM") upon which the narrative reaches a triumphant climax: the chant replaces the implied limits of the Western literary word with ethnic possibilities which are inherent in the black religious tradition and in the music that draws upon that tradition.

Finally, the very development of these tensions implies a certain sense of movement, the kind of progressive movement that is the theme of the last story, "Answers in Progress." The futuristic possibilities of the idea of progress are underlined by the science fiction format: aliens have invaded earth and are busy searching for jazz record albums. The search allows the narrator to introduce descriptive vignettes on black music as it is introduced to the invaders: they "dug the hell out of it. . . . Boooo — Iiiiiiooooooo. . .daaaa ahhhhh" (p. 131). There is an element of irony in Baraka's science fiction structure, for science as the extension of a rigidly technological culture is again his target here; and on this basis science is contrasted with the cultural and ethnic dimensions—the completeness—that Baraka usually attributes to black music. The traditional image of the superintelligent alien in science fiction is important here, because in this case the superintelligence identifies itself very closely with Baraka's ideal of wholeness rather than with a purely scientific standard.

In (American) social terms that ethnic ideal and its related art forms are really alien. They are also the promise of the future as Baraka envisages it: black music, black language, and their associated cultural values are the "answers" to the moral corruptions of American society and to the traditional disadvantages of blacks within that society. They are integral to the development of a new black spirit. Here, as in his political essays, Baraka has redefined the society's prevailing concept of progress, emphasizing progress as human growth rather than merely socioeconomic and scientific "development." Baraka's choice of narrative format invests this theme with a certain irony. The science fiction mode which is the product of white, technological societies and which seldom, if ever, deals with nonwhite experiences has been exploited by Baraka to defend and honor the culture of blacks in a subversively nationalistic sense.

Baraka's subversion of the science fiction mode is, therefore, both literary and political in its implications. The rejection of a self-centered technology is implicit in that subversion, and by extension there is also the repudiation of literary traditions in which form and technique are treated as self-sufficient, self-contained entities. Consequently the final story of *Tales* turns away, even more decisively than a work like "The Screamers," from prose fiction as strictly literary form to a narrative structure that incorporates the sounds as well as symbolic significance of black music. And this structure simultaneously incorporates the rhythms of spoken speech and physical movement (walking, for example) to enforce a sense of new beginnings within the community from which these non-literary forms originate: "walk on out through sunlight life, and know/ we're on the go/ for love/ to open/ our lives" (p. 129).

Henceforth Baraka's personal "answers in progress" as a writer will lie primarily in poetry and drama, the two genres in which he has been continuously active throughout his career, and which for reasons that we shall be exploring seem more congenial to his personal quest for the satisfactory synthesis of political activism and literary form. But although Baraka's quest is still in "progress" after 1967, it is doubtful that he ever comes as *consistently* close to that synthesis as he does in the short-story form, especially the kind of synthesis that allows him to combine the fervor of moral vision with excellence of design and execution.

CHAPTER 5

Baraka as Poet

A S one of the genres in which he has always worked poetry closely
reflects the changes in Baraka's political development. The
early years (1957–1960) resulted in the first collection of poems,
Preface to a Twenty Volume Suicide Note (1961), in which the radical
protest against social and moral decay is integrated with signs of an
incipient ethnic revolt. And on this basis the volume is comparable
with Baraka's political essays of the same period. The ethnic themes
are more pronounced in his second collection, *The Dead Lecturer*
(1964) where the black American's plight assumes major significance
in its own right while continuing, as in the first collection, to symbol-
ize general social corruption.

Most of the poems in *The Dead Lecturer* were written between
1960 and 1961, but the works in the third collection, *Black Magic*
(1967), cover the early phases of Baraka's black nationalism. The
volume combines the search for a positive black awareness with an
increasingly ferocious assault on white racism and Western culture.
Here black nationalism celebrates blackness, but for the most part it
is a kind of collective self-flagellation—that same scourging of self-
hatred which dominates *Dante's Hell* and *Tales*. The celebration of
black culture and identity is the sustaining theme of the next three
collections, *It's Nation Time* (1970), *In Our Terribleness* (1970), and
Spirit Reach (1972). Of these only two, *In Our Terribleness* and *Spirit
Reach*, are substantial enough to warrant detailed study here. Finally
his socialist phase is represented by *Hard Facts* (1975), a severely
limited body of poetry (in terms of quality and quantity) which adds
nothing to Baraka's achievement as poet or to his socialist perspectives, and which will, therefore, not be examined in this study.

As in other aspects of Baraka's writing the ideological shifts that are
evident in the poetry go hand in hand with a fundamental theme that
remains constant throughout: that is, whether he is inspired by a
vague radical outrage or by ethnic revolutionism Baraka's insights are

always rooted in a deep-seated contempt for what he sees as the defects of Western culture as a whole, and American society in particular. Moreover, despite the increasing alienation from all aspects of white America and the West, the poetry continues to show signs of Baraka's early association with nonblack artists. These artists include the "projective" school of poetry which influenced him during his Greenwich Village years. Advocates of projective verse emphasize the writing of poetry as an apparently spontaneous rather than obviously deliberate process, one in which the written word strives to approximate the rhythms of spoken speech. And in this process the poet's images are significant in vaguely suggestive ways rather than as explicit or concrete forms of illustrating an idea.[1] The projective approach to images clearly falls within the Imagist tradition, and Baraka's indebtedness to both is exemplified in his first collection by a work like "Turncoat" where the images owe their "significance" and unity primarily to the rhythms of the spoken word and to the vague evocation of a particular mood. In this instance the mood is one of gloom in a depressingly mechanical atmosphere of steel structures: "The steel fibrous slant & ribboned glint/of water. The Sea. Even my secret speech is moist/with it. When I am alone & brooding, locked in/ with dull memories & self-hate" (p. 26).[2]

In addition, a work like "Black Dada Nihilismus" (*The Dead Lecturer*) demonstrates the influence of the dadaist movement in Baraka's poetry, especially to the degree that such a movement encouraged a certain sense of unorthodoxy in the approach to structure and use of language. Thus the dadaists' emphasis on formlessness amounts to a rebellion against overly formalized approaches to art; and this emphasis is clearly a precursor to the criteria of the projective school that included Baraka and other "beat" poets in its numbers during the 1950s.[3] But as usual, Baraka does not simply borrow these techniques. The inherited forms and approaches to poetry are integrated, over the years, with the changes in his style and political ideology. The colloquial format and imagistic structures which he had developed as a member of the projective school easily adapted themselves to the oral modes of black American culture (the speech and the songs) and to the improvisational "free" forms of contemporary jazz. Similarly, the deliberately antiformal or "formless" poems that are encouraged by the dadaist heritage are comparable with those later works in which Baraka's aesthetic and social rebellion, as black nationalist, expresses itself.

But despite the consistency with which he successfully adapts inherited forms, Baraka's achievement as a poet is uneven. The effects of his "associationist" images are often brilliant, the use of sounds and rhythm is frequently innovative; but despite this his style can be surprisingly monotonous. The monotony results, paradoxically, from the poet's excessive reliance on the kind of images that "Turncoat" exemplifies. What is basically a stimulating approach to the writing of poetry sometimes bogs down because of lack of control. And as a result of this excess too much of Baraka's poetry reads like an extended version of "Turncoat."

The poetry also suffers from another kind of excess. As in the essays Baraka's criticism of social institutions and political groups often degenerates into mere name-calling. The attacks on white racists and on racism are self-justifying enough. But here, as elsewhere in his writings, Baraka weakens his case by being less precise than he should be in distinguishing between the barbarities of certain groups and the perilous notion that some groups are inferior simply because they exist. And at times his attacks on homosexuality and miscegenation are merely scurrilous without any demonstrated justification. In poems that lend themselves to this kind of scurrility, that analytical incisiveness which he often employs to brilliant effect gives way to vituperation. And the kinds of ideological excesses that often mar the black nationalist poetry completely negate the usefulness of *Hard Facts* as a sample of socialist poetry: here the poems are little more than a collection of ideological banalities and hackneyed name-calling; and as a consequence they lack even the flawed promise of Baraka's socialist drama.

I   Preface to a Twenty Volume Suicide Note

The scurrilities and general lack of control are a major drawback in the later collections, especially the black nationalist and socialist verse. But, despite the monotony that plagues the style of the first two volumes they remain Baraka's most consistently successful collections of poetry. His moral outrage and ethnic rebelliousness are enhanced rather than compromised by that sense of imaginative (rather than merely inhibiting) control which is progressively lacking in subsequent volumes. In *Preface to a Twenty Volume Suicide Note* the poet's anger is inspired by the familiar revulsion at American society as a moral wasteland and cultural wilderness. At the same time this perception of America is linked with a broader and pervasive skepticism about the human condition as a whole.

The title poem of the collection is therefore both specifically cultural and universal. The work is a vision of life as a kind of death, as a slow but inexorable process of dying that is both physical and spiritual. The adult persona of the poem goes mechanically through the repetitions of living (running for a bus, walking the dog, watching the night sky, and so forth); and this very repetitiveness encourages a sense of spiritual death in his world, a world in which no one sings any more. Then having developed the familiar portrait of disillusioned adulthood, the poet offers what appears at first glance to be the familiar contrast with childhood as an image of innocence and promising vitality. One night the persona hears his young daughter talking to someone in her room, but on opening the door he finds no one there—only "she on her knees, peeking into/ Her own clasped hands" (*Preface*, 5).

The childhood image is invested with a finely developed sense of ironic ambiguity that undercuts the initial image of old, time-worn contrasts between adult decay and childhood innocence. On the one hand the image of the praying child is a reminder of that spiritual vitality and that imaginative power which allow the child to transform the godhead into a playmate and confidante, into someone who remains invisible to the unperceptive imagination of the jaded adult. And on this basis prayer itself has become an intimate exchange between the child and the world of her imagination. But on the other hand, her "peeking" suggests a deliberate game of make believe, one calculated to relieve the tedium of bedtime prayers which have become the child's counterpart to the adult's world of mechanical repetition and empty forms. On both counts, the childhood image is associated with death. The impression of genuine innocence is tempered by the sobering awareness that the process of life-as-death will inevitably transform the praying child from imaginative spirit into the unseeing adulthood of her father's world. The suspicion that the bedtime prayer may already be a repetitive childhood ritual confirms that the child's existence has already been shaped by the process of life-as-death, that, indeed, to participate—however actively and imaginatively—in the life of the wasteland, is to engage in a suicide of sorts.

The idea of the wasteland is fairly specific and urgent in this collection of poetry. This is largely because there are so many unmistakable echoes of T. S. Eliot's *The Waste Land* in some of the poems, especially in "Roi's Blues" and in the three works grouped under the common title, "From an Almanac." Lee A. Jacobus's thoughtful reading of these works has already illuminated the young Baraka's indebtedness to Eliot's wasteland themes and imagery—especially the overview of moral decay, images of social fragmentation, the use of the seasons as symptoms of moral disruption, and the general search for a regenerative idealism in both poets. The death figure of the hanged man appears in Baraka's second "Almanac" poem, as it does in *The Waste Land*, and in "Roi's Blues" Baraka echoes the opening lines of *The Waste Land* by emphasizing the morally symbolic ravages of winter and the subsequent promise of renewed life in spring. As Jacobus points out, the wasteland of Eliot's poetry derives much of its emotional impact from the fact that it is always being contrasted, implicitly and otherwise, with an ideal moral order from which the human condition has been gradually separated but to which the poet is still committed; but on the other hand, Baraka's social vision is intensified by his rejection of the traditional (Christian) idealism to which Eliot appeals.[4]

Instead Baraka offers no salvation from the wasteland except in individually defined terms such as those that are represented by the self-affirmative quality of the blues tradition—the quality which, as we have seen, dominates the themes of growth in a work like *Dante's Hell*. Hence in "Roi's Blues" we discover that the very act of confronting and exploring the horrors of one's existence—the moral death and social decay of the poet's world—inspires and strengthens the individual capacity to transcend those horrors. In effect, Baraka unites with his borrowed images of the wasteland the distinctively affirmative traditions of the black American's blues.

On the other hand the failure or absence of these affirmative energies guarantees the inevitable triumph of the wasteland over one's moral perception and imaginative energies. This, clearly, is the fate of the adult in the title poem and it looms as a definite possibility for the ambiguous figure of the praying child. It has certainly been the fate of the protagonist (adopted from the *Thin Man* movies) in "The Death of Nick Charles," a work that is closely modelled at some points on Eliot's "The Love Song of Alfred J. Prufrock." The echoes of Eliot's work are fairly obvious in the images of ubiquitous winter fog, in the protagonist's deep sense of alienation and impotence, and in the inability of others to love and understand him.

In general Baraka's references to Eliot's work are more than imitation as such. Quite apart from the shared vision of experience as a wasteland, Baraka displays a profound skepticism—noted by critics like Jacobus—about the kind of Christian idealism which Eliot opposes to the wasteland reality. And the reader of Baraka's work is eventually persuaded that the white, Western Christianity of Eliot's moral vision is as much of a stumbling block to Baraka as is the wasteland which both poets denounce. As we have already noted in *Dante's Hell* Baraka's ambivalence toward a Western model like Eliot allows him to utilize the white poet's vision and images in order to develop his own moral perception, at the same time that he questions the cultural relevance and moral persuasiveness of his white model. On this basis Eliot's Anglo-Catholic idealism is the symptom of an alien tradition from which Baraka increasingly finds himself detached. As in so much of Baraka's work, the issue in *Preface* is not simply one of the conflict between the Western reality and the Western ideal. As we have already seen in the essays, Baraka as Greenwich Village radical and as black nationalist is often closer to the philosophical ideals of Western culture than he seems ready to acknowledge, but on a conscious level at any rate works like *Preface* reject both the philosophical idealism and the realities of the West in general and the United States in particular.

This skepticism about the nature of Western idealism specifically addresses itself to problems in American society in *Preface*. This is particularly true of those poems in which Baraka satirizes the kind of cultural values that he associates with the archetypes of the popular comic strips. Generally when Baraka examines the "all-American" innocence connoted by comic-strip heroes he concludes that here too the image of innocence might be ambiguous, even deceptive. The image often masks emotional unfulfillment and the kind of destructiveness that is symptomized by racial injustice. In "To a Publisher" the Peanuts child-heroes incarnate this emotional sterility. They are really grown-ups in juvenile disguises that fail to conceal the analogy with the adult world. Thus they will "turn out bad," will be inane disc jockeys, beatniks, or typical city-slickers. And Charlie Brown's love-hate relationship with Lucy reflects the emotional sterility in adult America (*Preface*, 18–19). In this sterile context violence and death, rather than love, have been sanctioned by the culture as forms of growth and awareness. The idealization of violence-as-manhood, for example, reflects a widespread approach to life as a kind of death. This is the kind of approach that Baraka perceives beneath the innocent veneer of comic-strip innocence. Consequently, to yearn for the comic-strip world of cowboys and space-age heroes, as the hero does in "Look for You Yesterday Here You Come Today," is really to long for death itself (*Preface*, 17).

The corruption of love in Baraka's comic-strip America is attributed to the culture's destructive dichotomies between reason and feeling, the kind of dichotomy that Baraka explores in "In Memory of Radio." The poem is actually a study in contrasts, parodying the culture's conventional antithesis between reason and feeling, between a limited mathematical rationalism and emotional involvement. The rationalistic archetype in the poem is Mandrake the Magician, from whom the poet dissociates himself by pointedly disclaiming powers of hypnosis. The choice of Mandrake as symbol of rationalism is a striking one because the culture usually associates "magic" with the "occult" and other suspect modes of nonrational perception. But such a choice is effective precisely because it emphasizes the degree to which the obsession with a narrow rationalism has had the effect of surrounding "reason" with all the primitive mystique that the culture itself usually attributes to magic: in Western culture reason has become sacrosanct, a sacred cow that is defended by its worshippers with an *irrational* fervor. Thus the "magic" of radio technology connotes the impressive nature of the technology in its own right; but, turning the culture's pejorative use of the term "magic" against itself, Baraka's poem defines the "magic" of radio as a symptom of the irrational basis on which the culture perceives the achievements of technological reason.

On both counts Mandrake therefore represents the scientific logic that made possible the technological "magic" of radio. The figure's familiar attributes (the hypnotic gesture and the powers of invisibility) reinforce that sense of a wonderful ("magical") emotional intimacy which is intrinsic to the experience of listening to radio: the listener develops private relationships with radio characters precisely because the latter's invisibility demands an imaginative participation from the listener, and thereby enhances the intimacy of the relationships. But "magic" in this sense is really part of the culture's make-believe innocence. In retrospect it is obviously a fraud, a pretended closeness, which does not really compensate for the isolation and divisiveness that the culture encourages by virtue of its fearfully puritanic and narrowly rationalistic responses to love and involvement. Seen in this light, even the sequence of the programs to which the poet listened in his youth becomes ironically revealing: "Red Lantern" is followed by "Let's Pretend."

Radio therefore represents a pretended involvement and intimacy. The pretence is the more incongruous because the scientific rationalism that made radio a possibility has contributed to the inhibition of emotional experience in the culture. Accordingly love has been transformed, becoming an evil rather than creative experience. The transformation has all the connotations of that evil "magic" which the culture abhors: the "magical" reversal of the spelling ("evol") reflects the real evil—the evil of denying love (*Preface*, 12).

The very sterility of the society's emotional experience encourages a certain need for heroes, for heroic archetypes with whom the individual comic-strip fan can establish a make-believe intimacy that substitutes for the absence of love in the culture. Indeed the point has been reached where we are capable of loving only heroes who can scale the walls of social division—in our imaginations at least—in "The Death of Nick Charles." And because this kind of hero-worship is a self-protective, compensatory defence in an unloveable world, then it evokes a certain sympathy in both "The Death of Nick Charles" and "Look for You Yesterday."

But insofar as this hero-worship is a collective, continuing pretence it really belongs to what Baraka perceives as the destructively false myths of American innocence. R. W. B. Lewis has accounted for the tradition of American innocence in his analysis of what he calls the American Adam, a new kind of hero who embodies a new set of human ideals in the New World. The American Adam represents a vision of innocence that is really illusory, Lewis emphasizes, but "without the illusion, we are conscious, no longer of tradition, but simply and coldly of the burden of history." [5] But while Lewis is prepared to accept the illusions that are inherent in this tradition of American innocence, Baraka sees these illusions as symptoms of deep flaws in the very notion of American innocence.

Consequently the attack on comic-strip images of innocence in a work like *Preface* stems from the belief that the myths and images of American innocence have never been devoted, in the culture's history, to the propagation of ideals, however illusory these might be. Far from being idealistic images opposed to the "burden of history," or to unmitigated evil, Baraka's comic-strip heroes embody the real corruptions—stunted emotions, violence, ingrained habits of pretence and deception—that are endemic to America as wasteland. On the one hand Lewis's enthusiasm for the cowboy archetype and its literary counterparts leads him to declare that the "greatest moment" in James Fenimore Cooper occurs in *Deerslayer* where the hero passes "the trial of honor, courage, and self-reliance" by killing—a fit of violence that Lewis, curiously enough, describes in erotic terms: the hero and his antagonist fire simultaneously at each other, and it is "like a kiss" (*The American Adam*, p. 104). On the other hand, Baraka attacks the comic-strip archetype precisely because he is repelled by this kind of equation between violence, manhood and sexuality, perceiving such an equation as a moral and emotional perversion that is confirmed rather than transcended by the "innocent" archetypes of America's cultural myths. What Lewis sees as an innocent transcendence strikes Baraka simply as the symptom of a deathlike, and deadly, tradition.

Consequently, in "Look for You Yesterday" the ideal connotations of innocence are undermined by the historical brutality (cowboys, for example) of the comic-strip archetype. To yearn for the comic-book world of youthful idealism is therefore to long for an innocent heroism that never existed:

> Where is my space helmet, I sent for it
> 3 lives ago . . . when there were box tops.
> What has happened to box tops??
> O, God . . . I must have a belt that glows green
> in the dark. Where is my Captain Midnight decoder??
> I can't understand what Superman is saying!
> THERE *MUST* BE A LONE RANGER!!! (*Preface*, 17)

Superman is the mythic symbol of that invincible goodness which the persona associates with the innocent myths of comic-strip child-hood. But the figure is also the stereotype of (white) racial supremacy here, a being whose distinctively Caucasian virility enforces tradi-tional equations of purity with whiteness. His unintelligibility in this context therefore reflects the persona's growing awareness of the noncommunication between black and white in the real, as opposed to the mythically innocent, America. And ethnic barriers like these are part of an emotional wasteland in which emotional fulfillment amounts to nothing more than a "maudlin nostalgia" for figures of violence and death. Hence the disillusioned persona thinks of Tom Mix as a depressingly real social archetype, "dead in a Boston Night-club/ before I realized what happened" (*Preface*, 16). In more per-sonal terms, the death of Tom Mix represents the death of that childhood innocence which allowed the cowboy archetype to exist as a positive image of goodness in the persona's consciousness. The dead Tom Mix and the dead innocence of the narrator are one and the same. As for the Lone Ranger, he is also a symptom of the narrator's cultural milieu and subjective experience. And he is moribund:

> My silver bullets all gone
> My black mask trampled in the dust
> & Tonto way off in the hills
> moaning like Bessie Smith (*Preface*, p. 18).

As another white superman the Lone Ranger is linked here with the traditional victims of white supremacy. His personality is defined in relation to the nonwhite's humiliation. The trampled black mask (the black American) is crucial to the Lone Ranger's identity. So is Tonto, the "good Injun." Indeed, without these the Lone Ranger is unrecognizable. And in this regard he emphasizes the degree to which American culture as a whole, and the white American in particular, owe their very identity to a certain interaction with nonwhite groups that are traditionally brutalized or ignored by the society. However, at this time Baraka perceives the Lone Ranger and his kind as figures of decay, not simply because of the moral corruptions that they embody, but also because of the exposure of those racist traditions which spawned them. Time, like the movie-reel at a "western," is running out, and the dispossessed are no longer quiescent: "I hear the reel running out . . ./ the spectators are impatient for popcorn." The new impatience will not be fooled by the traditional facade of mythic innocence. Tonto and his black counterparts have deserted, and, in the language of the blues, their anger heightens the impression that time is running out for the Lone Ranger: "old envious blues feeling/ ticking like a big cobblestone clock" (*Preface*, 17).

These racial conflicts are not simply allegories of America's moral wasteland, although they do serve an allegorical function in *Preface* as a whole. They are also significant, in their own right, as reflections of Baraka's racial perception in this early collection of poetry. Nonwhites are therefore not simply victims of America's social system as a whole. They are also accessories to their own victimization by participating, as the narrator has done in his youth, in the myths of American innocence. Accordingly, the ethnic tensions of "Look for You Yesterday" are not simply external. They also represent, on an internal level, the black American's double consciousness, the contradictions between a nonwhite ethnicity and the acceptance of white cultural myths. Conversely, the demise of the Lone Ranger heralds an incipient cultural awakening and the destruction of white cultural values *within* the black psyche. The ethnic and cultural changes envisaged in "Look for You Yesterday" and similar poems are not on the scale of Baraka's later themes of rebellion and revolution. As in much of his earlier work these poems envision black ethnicity within rather than in opposition to the idea of American culture as a whole. Black nationalism and the search for a Pan-African sensibility are to be the concerns of subsequent volumes of poetry. For the time being the African heritage is something of a foreign irrelevance ("Notes for a Speech") that cannot challenge the poet's acceptance of America as home (*Preface*, 47).

II   The Dead Lecturer

The themes of ethnic identity are progressively more intense in Baraka's second collection. These themes, together with the continuing satire on scientific rationalism, dominate *The Dead Lecturer*. Both sets of themes are effectively integrated in "Green Lantern's Solo" in which the institutions of white America represent intellectual and racial attitudes that have traditionally contributed to the brutalization of black America. The poem's setting is a world without passion, one that is symbolized by urine which "scatters/as steel." It is a world of incongruities where lyric poets are so divorced from feeling that they have never had orgasms, where social critics are detached from society itself, and where supposedly human institutions are really dehumanizing. Religion is a mere abstraction, an "irreducible, constantly correcting, dogmatic economy/ of the soul" (pp. 67–70).[6]

The system also has disturbing ethnic implications for Baraka, both because it victimizes the black outsider and because it represents the limited humanity that blacks inherit when they choose to be integrated with such a system. On the whole the ethnic themes of *The Dead Lecturer* represent a growing resistance to Western intellectualism as the instrument of white racism and the source of a destructive pattern of black self-hatred. Hence the persona of "I Substitute for the Dead Lecturer" admits that in accepting rigidly intellectual norms he has destroyed his racial integrity and, in the process, his humanity. In recognizing the limitations of this intelligence he admits that he has become a mere death-figure—a "stewed black skull,/ an empty cage of failure" (*Dead*, 60).

Painful as it is such a recognition marks the beginning of the persona's return to human and ethnic integrity. This is the kind of return that is underway in "Green Lantern's Solo" where the narrator is in full flight from his self-hatred: "I break and run" after having lived a life surrounded by "the smelly ghosts of wounded intellectuals" (*Dead*, 67). Similarly in "Rhythm & Blues" the intellectually emancipated black sees the "rational" systems of his society as they really affect human beings. Economics kill human beings. The idea of technological "progress" is a sham because "new" creations are really extensions of the old malaise. And the political system is merely a death-machine, like the economic system: "the old man dead in his/ tired factory; election machines chime quietly his fraudulent faith" (*Dead*, 45–46). Conversely "A Contract" chastises blacks who persist in their loyalties to the system. They are Uncle Toms whose racial self-hatred involves a self-destructive psychic violence: they have been killed "in white fedora hats" (*Dead*, 11).

The violent connotations of the Uncle Tom figure are striking here because Baraka perceives the figure as a stereotype that has been perpetuated by white society to destroy black humanity—with the complicity of blacks. Similarly, in "A Poem for Willie Best" the black actor, "Sleep 'n' Eat," is linked with violence. He is the victim of violence, one who has been crucified by the stereotypes of society, but who is now screaming "into existence" (p. 19). The Uncle Tom's scream introduces another dimension of the figure as it is handled by Baraka in this work and in *The Dead Lecturer* as a whole. It is a scream of agony by the black victim of racism; and it is simultaneously a violent affirmation of a new sense of self. This ambiguity emphasizes the degree to which the violent rhetoric and postures of black self-discovery are themselves responding to the psychic violence of white racism (and acquiescent Uncle Tomism). Here Baraka's Uncle Tom is no longer a one-dimensional figure of acquiescence. He is breaking out of the subhuman criteria through which he and others have defined his identity. As a result of this self-affirmation the "renegade" (i.e., antiblack) posture of the Uncle Tom is becoming a mask rather than a reality. And that mask conceals a different kind of "renegade," the black whose uncompromising racial pride earns him that title from reactionary whites:

> A renegade
> behind the mask. And even
> the mask, a renegade
> disguise. Black skin
> and hanging lip. (*Dead*, 26)

Baraka's revolt against western rationalism also involves the poet's increasing preoccupation with the nature of his art. Baraka associates with limited rationalsim those aesthetic norms which he perceives as the dominant factors in art and criticism in Western culture. In "The Politics of Rich Painters" these norms are integral parts of limited social systems in the culture as a whole. The art of rich painters is bloodless. It caters to a narrow notion of taste that excludes emotional response. And since it it fails to be fully human such art is merely "another name for liar." Finally this limited art is intimately involved with the dominant socioeconomic system—with the "commerce" of a "decadent economy" (*Dead*, 32–33).

"A Political Poem" also takes up the attack on commercially attractive but spiritually limited art. Poetry, in the poet's society, is simply another symptom of the culture's negation of feeling. The standard, acceptable poetry is therefore the "noxious game of reason, saying, 'No, No/ you cannot feel' " (*Dead*, 74). "Black Dada Nihilismus" is the most ambitious and successful of these attacks, in *The Dead Lecturer*, on the limited aesthetics of excessive rationalism (*Dead*, 61–64). The poem succeeds in part because Baraka blends his aesthetic revolt so well with his themes of ethnic rebellion. Black violence considered either as reprehensible and criminal (rape and murder) or as calculated rebellion still amounts to retaliation against an established order that prizes its own rational norms above the feelings of its victims. But Black Dada's criminality is disturbing in a deep sense because it is the symptom and product of a racial caste system that is secured by political and socioeconomic systems. With telling irony Baraka manages to argue, in effect, that the emotionally limited sense of order that is so prized by the established systems has actually been the direct cause of psychic and social disorder.

But Black Dada's violence is not perceived in exclusively criminal terms. It also smacks of heroism, a deliberate rebelliousness that links him with a long history of covert and overt resistance to racial injustice. In turn this kind of creative resistance is linked with the prevailing aesthetic issue of the poem. Black Dada's name obviously recalls the dadaist revolt in art. Black Dada's ethnic rebellion is the political counterpart of the dadaists' calculated use of "formlessness" as a means of revolting against excessive, rationalistically defined formalism. And, by extension, the black poet who combines the rebellious ethnic perspective with the aesthetic criteria of the dadaists is engaged in his art as total experience—art as an act of rebellion against limiting social systems and against limited notions of artistic creativity. The "nihilism" of ethnic violence and dadaist outrage alike has become a creative process.

At this point "Black Dada Nihilismus" reflects Baraka's skill in blending archetypes within the persona of the poet himself. The poet *is* Black Dada. His art embodies aesthetic and social concerns. And in the very process of synthesizing the aesthetic and the social in the person of the poet the poem rejects those intellectual standards which insist upon keeping such concerns separate. Considered in these terms Black Dada represents a certain self-consciousness on Baraka's part about the role of the poet and the significance of his art. This self-awareness allows Baraka to deal with the poet-persona as social archetype. Thus in "The Liar" the poet's work is a public statement. He is one who is "loud" about the "birth" of his ways, "publicly redefining" each change in his soul (p. 79).

The frank autobiographical reference in this work is clear enough. But more interesting is the fact that either as autobiographical statement or as definition of the poet's role (or both), Baraka is emphasizing that the poet's role, or art, is representational rather than wholly private and self-indulgently alienated. On the whole the art of Baraka's poet is dual in nature. On one level it is private, dealing with his soul's experience—with his "ways." But on another level it is simultaneously public, not simply by the act of public statement but also because the statement and the private experience that it describes are of public significance. The poet is a social archetype. Similarly in "The Dance" the art of the dance and the analogous rhythms of the poet's language are ambiguous. There is one sense in which the artist's medium is of public significance. But in another sense it is intensely private: it expresses feelings and describes things that "I alone create" (*Dead*, 71).

This emphasis on the uniqueness of the created "thing" and on the creative process itself brings us to another aspect of the ambiguity that Baraka attributes to art here. Each art is expressive and symbolic of a public or collective experience, and in this respect all art forms are interchangeable with each other at certain points of expressiveness. The dancer's art therefore replaces words. The poet's verbal and tonal structures are integrated with the body language of the dancer's rhythms. The dancer's consciousness of the body is paralleled by the poet's self-consciousness about the verbal structures with which he explores feeling and sensuous experience. But notwithstanding these relationships between art and society, and between the arts themselves, each art form and each work of art is stamped with its own uniqueness. This sense of uniqueness has two main sources. First, it is the result of the fact that art proceeds, in part, from the private self and separate identity of the artist ("I alone"). Secondly, it is the logical outcome of the artist's conviction that despite the ideal of committed art, the artist is separate by virtue of the peculiar, or unusual, nature of art as creative process in an essentially uncreative world ("I alone create").

III   Black Magic: Collected Poetry 1961–1967

In poems like "The Dance" and in *The Dead Lecturer* as a whole Baraka maintains a delicate balance between the artist's uniqueness and the ideal of social commitment. On this basis the collection is a significant example of the tension between his role as artist and his role as political activist, between writing as straightforward political statement and art as a unique but politically committed design. As we have already shown, this tension persists throughout Baraka's career. After *The Dead Lecturer* his poetry often takes the form of a bombastic directness, but the very fact that he persists in the medium is an indication that he continues to distinguish between poetic art, even of a baldly dogmatic kind, and expository statement. *Black Magic*, the third collection of poems, is more uneven than *The Dead Lecturer* precisely because, in practice at least, Baraka's poetry loses some of the tensions which account for the fine balance of art and commitment in the preceding volume.

Baraka himself minimizes the achievements of his first two volumes, preferring to see them, in his preface to *Black Magic*, merely as symptoms of sickness, signs of the "whiteness" that he had inherited from European "abstraction and disjointedness." Conversely, he is more satisfied with the three sections that comprise *Black Magic*: "Sabotage" as an exposé of America's social ills, "Target Study" as the analysis of methods needed to eradicate these ills, and "Black Art" as the expression of a new ethnic spirit that separates blacks from the society. Baraka's description of the collection is somewhat surprising. It smacks of that very rigidity which he repeatedly attributes to Western rationalism, for it ignores the degree of thematic overlapping and repetition throughout the volume as a whole.

He is more convincing in the choice of title. The title assumes a special significance in light of the volume's recurrent attacks on excessive rationalism. "Black magic" has usually been associated, in white, Western culture, with evil and destructiveness; but now Baraka's poetry transforms it into a beneficial and creative process. It is both an ethnic and aesthetic power, attacking rationalistic systems in the culture as tools of economic and racial exploitation, and rejecting overly formalistic approaches to art. The idea of magic in both ethnic and aesthetic terms is therefore intrinsically bound up with the experience of transformation: self-hatred is replaced by ethnic pride and art-for-art's sake gives way to art as responsive and committed design. Magic, the very essence of "irrationality" and disorder, in rationalistic terms, is now the symbol of a new, rebellious anti-rationalism. It is a rebellion in which exclusive reliance on objective logic is discarded in favor of the synthesis of reason and feeling, form and substance, in both society and art.

Although we may cavil at Baraka's rather rigid distinctions between the sections of *Black Magic* those distinctions do have some validity. While it is easy to find poems attacking American society as a whole throughout the volume, it is in the "Sabotage" section that this theme is predominant—especially in poems like "Three Modes of History and Culture" (p. 3), "A Poem Some People Will Have to Understand" (p. 6), "The New World" (p. 22) and "Square Business" (pp. 29–30). Indeed at this point in Baraka's poetry the theme is decidedly *deja vu*. The insights into the American wasteland are familiar and tediously repetitive—inhuman technology and lack of feeling ("Three Modes" and "Square Business") or the culture's false and guilty images of innocence ("The New World"). And this thematic staleness is complemented by the repetitive style.

As usual the attacks on society are followed by the familiar echoes of ethnic reaction. These echoes dominate "Target Study" which differs from *Preface* and *The Dead Lecturer* in that the ethnic reaction is now decidedly separatist. "Friday" is a sustained series of invectives against America that concludes with a passionate cry for black separation: "You are strong. Leave them. Leave/ them" (p. 53). "I Don't Love You" depicts white society in a series of negative images, especially the mirror image ("whiteface glass") that has encouraged blacks to reject their racial identity in favor of beloved white standards. But the "don'ts" of this "white" hell are eventually succeeded by the concluding declaration, "I don't love you" (p. 55). Despite its negative emphasis the declaration is actually the positive affirmation of that ethnic self-love which enforces a sense of ethnic separateness. "Return of the Native" also moves from the negative statement to the positive celebration. Harlem, the subject of the poem, is ambiguous: it is both beautiful and violent, a place of pain and love. The poem's structure moves from the description of Harlem's ugly sides ("Harlem is vicious/ modernism") to the positive declaration of love: "suffer/ in joy, that our lives/ are so familiar" (p. 108).

Interestingly enough those poems which concentrate on a sense of new ethnic spirit are more imaginatively executed. There is a freshness in language and an innovative approach to form which lift such works above the pedestrian level of most protest poems in *Black Magic*. Moving from the repetitive themes of white racism to the subject of a black awakening seems to have given fresh impetus to Baraka's imaginative energies. In this vein, the theme of an ethnic awakening owes its air of urgency to the repeated call on which "Friday" concludes ("Leave them"). The use of the negative ("I don't love you") as a positive statement is more than a bit of syntactic cleverness. The rhetorical shift from the overt negative to an implied positive is analogous to a comparable shift within the ethnic consciousness that the poem describes—a shift from an obvious, long-standing self-hatred to an implied, tentative racial pride. The poem's rhetorical structure has therefore been integrated with the poet's theme of psychic growth. There is a comparable integration in "Return of the Native." The progression from a bleak, despairing image of Harlem to the affirmation of love—even in suffering—is effective because it is linked with the tradition of the blues. More specifically, Baraka draws here, as he does so frequently in his works, on the blues tradition of deriving a sense of triumph from the very act of confronting pain: in immersing oneself in the suffering of Harlem, then, one discovers the special love for ethnic and cultural roots.

The blues idiom is more explicit in "I Am Speaking of Future Good-ness and Social Philosophy" (pp. 99–101), but the effect is quite similar. The assertion of an untrammelled black pride is analogous to the kind of spiritual affirmation that is the hallmark of the blues: "So we must become Gods./ Gigantic black ones" (p. 99). But what makes this poem one of the most impressive works in the "Target Study" section is the felicity with which Baraka blends the blues, as a series of declarative statements, with rhythms that recall the chant of the sorcerer—the black magician:

> And then, with steel
>   with bricks
>   with garbage
>   dogs, purposes
>   madness, tranquility,

                    weakness, strength, deadness. . . .
                                (these aint clams
                    you eatin
                    an ol' nigger
                    say, overhearing
                    this poem in my bowels,
                                ain't clams
                                dad.)
            In short everything that is magical, will respond, in men,
                                        if we
                    have the code
                    to their hearts. (pp. 99–100)

In effect the "magic" of ethnic and moral change is integrated with the
"magical" triumph of self over suffering in the blues tradition.

On the whole the "Target Study" section of *Black Magic* develops
the idea of ethnic pride with the kind of positive emphasis that
foreshadows Baraka's subsequent themes of black separatism in the
"Black Art" section. The emerging separatism of "Target Study" goes
hand in hand with the celebration of the powers of the human spirit.
In "Confirmation," for example, spirit is the essence of the universe
and each individual is a manifestation of that universal spirituality:
"The world is the most perfect thing in the soul. The world/ is a soul,
and we are souls if we remember the murmurs of the spirit" (p. 50).
And since the individual is essentially spiritual, then the celebration
of spiritual qualities, on ethnic and other grounds, is actually the
celebration of individual self. It is an act of self-love of the kind which
dominates the themes of the "Black Art" section.

In keeping with the interweaving of themes throughout *Black
Magic* as a whole, the subject of ethnic self-love is often juxtaposed in
this section with the familiar issue of black self-hatred. "The Deadly
Eyes" (p. 142) is an example of this juxtaposition. Self-love as such is
really dramatized by emphasizing its opposite. Hence the destructiveness of racial self-hatred is underscored by the jolting image of a
junkie pumping drugs into the veins: when accepted and internalized
by self-hating blacks the racial attitudes of whites are akin to "white
filth/ jamming thru my veins." Unfortunately, the handling of these
ethnic themes does not often match the level of even the relatively
slight "Deadly Eyes"—especially when the emphasis is on self-
hatred. As with the repeated attacks on white racism, Baraka's
themes of self-hatred suffer from excessive repetition throughout

Black Magic as a whole. For example, "Race" (p. 122), really adds nothing new to Baraka's subject. And despite its intrinsic merits "Human to Spirit: Humanism for Animals" (pp. 201–204) does not really go beyond "I Am Speaking of Future Good-ness and Social Philosophy." The thematic interweaving of the blues, magic, and black "soul" culture is identical in both works. And in both poems the techniques of magical chant are very similar.

Here in *Black Magic*, as in *The Dead Lecturer*, some of the more innovative and interesting poems are those which deal in a creatively self-conscious way with the nature and function of poetry itself, and which, in the process, address themselves to the identity of the artistic imagination in general. Admittedly the well-known poem, "Black Art," addresses these issues in a limited rather than complex way. It is vociferous rather than imaginative, very often confusing racial invective with racial protest and relying on heavy-handed dogma instead of imaginative forms. But "Black Art" is the exception rather than the rule among poems dealing with the poetic imagination in *Black Magic*. Indeed the frequency with which Baraka returns to this issue suggests that as he becomes more and more involved in political activism, as a black nationalist, he is increasingly fascinated with the nature of the creative process and with the peculiar significance of art in a revolutionary context.

The link between Baraka's black nationalism and his interest in the artistic imagination is most apparent in the "Black Art" section of *Black Magic*. That tension which we noted in *The Dead Lecturer* between art as design and art as committed statement is still evident here. But the sense of a delicate balance between both aspects of the artistic role is missing in *Black Magic*. Instead there is a more pressing insistence on the political nature and purpose of any "valid" art. But this insistence is not developed in an absolute, single-minded way. In the very process of emphasizing the need for art as a form of political statement even a limited poem like "Black Art" implies that there is a real distinction between art and other forms of political statement: "Let the world be a Black Poem/ And Let All Black People Speak This Poem/Silently / or LOUD" (p. 117).

The ease with which the poet interchanges "world" and "poem" here is more apparent than real. For the actual need to establish intrinsic links between people and poetry implicitly recognizes the essential peculiarities of poetry, or art in general, as imaginative design. Moreover, the actual process of exploring the characteristics of *politically committed* poetry really isolates and highlights those special qualities which distinguish even such committed poetry—as artistic form. In this connection "Poem for HalfWhite College Students" is more than a harangue at naive young blacks and their (white) cultural models (Elizabeth Taylor, Richard Burton, and Steve McQueen). As a harangue the poem is a political act, and as such it exemplifies the political basis of Baraka's aesthetic views at this time. But, simultaneously, the harangue is not simply a matter of ideological content. It also represents a rather calculated and crucial sense of artistic design. As a traditionally oral form the harangue accommodates Baraka's typical attempts to create poetic and other literary forms by integrating literary techniques with oral modes. The poem is sound, sound as political act (the harangue) and as deliberately conceived, specially executed design. And as sound it competes with other artistic and political forms for the attention of Baraka's college audience: "Who are you, listening to me. . .?" (p. 120). Moreover, the poem challenges that audience to participate in the black cultural traditions of oral art, especially rhythm and blues. And in so doing Baraka is integrating the political "sounds" of the poem with the "sounds" of black America's traditional music. This is precisely the kind of integration that makes the poem both a political act and a deliberately contrived work of art.

"A School of Prayer" is a comparable work in that here too the sounds of ethnic consciousness are integral to the poet's self-conscious sense of poetic form as political sound: "black blood screaming. . . . We are so beautiful we talk at the same time" (p. 121). In "Ka 'Ba" that self-consciousness is more pronounced. The sounds of a positive ethnic awareness stimulate the need for the related sounds of political action, for the "sacred words" of a magically transforming political movement (p. 146). Here the image of magic is a unifying one because it emphasizes the possibilities of change at the same time that it represents that concept of the word as action which is central to Baraka's poetry at this stage. The magical word of transformation is, of course, the chant, the kind of chant that defines the nature of poetic form and political awareness in "I Am Speaking of Future Good-ness and Social Philosophy." Consequently in "The Spell" the entire poem itself is conceived as a spell, as a chant in which sound itself is intended to galvanize the listener into a special ("magical") kind of ethnic change: "The Spell The SPELL THE SPELLLLLLLLLLLLLL! (p. 147).

Baraka's increasing insistence on the intrinsic relationship between poetry as political sound and aesthetic form may be traced to a specific cause in his political philosophy. It is rooted in that ideal of spirituality which dominates his black nationalist writings, including the political essays that we have already examined. "Trespass Into Spirit" is therefore simply an extended chant, rising, falling and rising again on a series of sounds—"aa," "eah," "oo," "uu," and "aa" (p. 151). And as the title implies the chant, that is the poem, is a special invocation of the human spirit. Similarly, in "Part of the Doctrine" the title is combined with the dominant sounds of the poem (repetitions of "raise," "race," "raze," and "god"). In the case of "god" the chanted repetition of the word is accelerated until it becomes one continuous sound "GODGODGODGODGODGODGODGOD"). This combination, and the accompanying repetitions, have the effect of making the poetic form more than the illustration of a doctrine. The form itself becomes the sound, and thereby the emotional experience, of the doctrine. The poem is "part of the doctrine," not simply because of its theme but by virtue of its form. In a work like this the fusion of poetry as political statement and poetry as tonal form is complete (p. 200).

Interestingly enough this kind of fusion underscores the continuous or evolutionary nature of Baraka's career as a writer. Hence the black nationalist separatism that he espouses at this stage and his interest in poetry as sound or tonal form may be traced back to his earliest period as a poet. For in that early period, as we may recall, he and other members of the Greenwich Village "beat" generation were influenced by the "projective" school of poetry in which images and sound are the essence of the poet's form and meaning. Indeed, given the revolutionary rhetoric of change which constitutes the "sounds" of Baraka's black nationalist poetry it is a striking fact that these works tend to reinforce a strong sense of tradition, encouraging a return to old customs and traditions rather than actually advocating radical reconstruction based on brand new blueprints.

This apparent paradox is partly based on the essentially continuous nature of Baraka's temperament as poet and political thinker, assuring that the techniques and philosophy of the moment bear the unmistakable marks of an earlier period in his development. But it is also linked with the significance of magic as both symbol and sound in his poetry. For magic is not simply an arbitrarily chosen emblem of Baraka's rebellion against a restrictively rationalistic culture. Magic is an appropriate vehicle for Baraka's rebellion because it harks back to a pretechnological age, one in which "magic," as both belief and practice, was an integral part of a homogenous world view. And that world view was homogenous because there were no rationalistically defined antitheses between the spiritual and nonspiritual, intellect and feeling.

It is also a world view that Baraka habitually attributes at this time to African cultures, for in *Black Magic* Africa is no longer the irrelevance that it was in *Preface to a Twenty Volume Suicide Note*. Now Africa is the major symbol of Baraka's black American nationalism. In this context, magic is both a weapon against white racism in the West and a means of affirming spiritual and moral values which Baraka attributes to pre-colonial Africa and which he now opposes to the rationalistic West. Hence in "Black People: This Is Our Destiny" Baraka declares that the "primitives" (as white Westerners are wont to term pretechnological, nonwhite cultures) are about to "civilize" the world (p. 199). The deliberate reversal of the cultural roles ("primitive" and "civilized"), as they are usually defined by white Westerners, underscores Baraka's "magical" transformation of words and political attitudes—the kind of transformation that is central to his posture as rebellious poet (i.e., black magician).

Consequently, in spite of those intellectual shortcomings which we have already noted in Baraka's black nationalism, his perception and handling of poetry at this time are fairly effective. Indeed the more successful poems in *Black Magic* are impressive because there is a convincing sense of integration—a compelling blend of magic as the essence of spirituality, magic as the chant of ethnic awakening, and magical chant as the sound, or tonal design, of politically committed poetry. Despite the obvious emphasis on straightforward political statement, then, the poems that reflect this blending do harmonize the ethical, the spiritual, and the political into a well-defined form. And that form is in itself an example of poetry as both aesthetic form and political statement. In turn this impression of a well-integrated poetic form exemplifies a central issue in Baraka's philosophical idealism as black nationalist: it is an example of that wholeness or completeness which Baraka envisages in an ideal society and in the individual consciousness within such a society.

This does not, of course, deny the more explicit politicizing with which Baraka's less imaginative poems attempt to define the nature of his art. The direct, frontal attack on American society in "Sabotage" is exemplified, in that section, by poems like "Houdini": the image of the junkie sniffing white powder is an obvious attack on the aesthetics of art-as-escape (art for art's sake) which the poet deplores in white culture (p. 7). In the same section "Gatsby's Theory of Aesthetics" is

actually an explicit prose description of poetry as meaning and feeling. Poetry is not a self-sufficient form, but the poet's political commitment, as well as his own process of growth (p. 41). "Gatsby's
Theory" is complemented by "Kenyatta Listening to Mozart," a
poem which deliberately invokes a sense of formlessness by relying
heavily on fractured syntax, typographical discontinuities, and images of movement or restiveness. This "formlessness" is implicitly
opposed to a rigid sense of form among those who insist upon the
purity of form for its own sake. But, ironically enough, this very
emphasis upon "formlessness" defines the structure of the poem as a
coherent thematic statement:

> A zoo of consciousness,
> cries and prowlings
> anywhere. Stillness,
> motion,
> beings that fly, beings
> that swim
> exchanging
> in-
> formation.
> Choice, and
> style,
> avail
> and are beautiful
> categories
> If you go
> for that. (p. 14)

The title of "Form Is Emptiness" is a more explicit statement of the
theme of "Kenyatta." The poem itself is a prolonged chant based on
the sound "aa" in "Rah," "Damballah," "Chakra" and other non-
Western deities or heroes:

> Raaaa
> aaaaaaaaaaaaaaaaaaaahhhhhhhhhhhhhhhh
> Allaaaaaaaaaaaaahhhhhhhhhhhh
> Dam
> Ballaaaaaaaaahhhhhhhhhhhh
> Chakra, the Buddha. . . . (p. 155)

Here, with remarkable economy, Baraka has succeeded in marshal-
ing together his basic themes in order to emphasize his aesthetic

preferences—religion and magic as ritualistic forms of spiritual and social wholeness, the magical, pretechnological nuances of the chant as antirationalistic sound, and the idea of poetry itself as sound. And the blending of these themes results in an integrated structure that is coherent and symptomatic of the poet's deliberate sense of design— at the very moment in which the poem as a whole rebels against the idea of formal design for its own sake. At the same time the idea of form for its own sake is actually associated, in an ironic way, with the work's seeming formlessness. Hence the *apparent* inanities of the poem's chants and its typographical idiosyncracies really constitute a parody of certain fads in which artistic "form" consists of random sounds, or visual configurations, without regard for meaning or moral commitment.

There is a telling irony here in the manner in which the poem reverses standard criticisms of committed art as "formless" statement and "mere" politics. Here any significant sense of form is dependent upon a coherent and tangible body of meaning. And, conversely, an excessive, self-contained preoccupation with form for its own sake— to the exclusion of meaning—results in an inane formlessness. The superb control with which Baraka achieves this ironic effect in "Kenyatta" and "Form Is Emptiness" contrasts with the unimaginative explicitness of "Sabotage" works like "Gatsby's Theory of Aesthetics." It must also be distinguished from the verbal and emotional excesses of the better-known "Black Art," which attempts to define the black aesthetic as a substitute for a "white" aesthetic. It may also be an unintended, but nonetheless significant, irony that the more successful poems depend on Baraka's skillful handling of language and structure—on his sense of artistic form—rather than on the intrinsic persuasiveness of his black nationalist aesthetics as such. And although such an irony might contradict Baraka's overt political aims in such poems, it does confirm the degree to which he retains a deep-seated sense of art as specially crafted design, even in the very act of emphasizing the crucial importance of art as political action.

IV   *The Later Poetry*

The interest in poetic art as form, albeit a politically committed form, persists in the poetry published after *Black Magic*. *In Our Terribleness* is a compelling example of this interest. Written and published at the peak of Baraka's black nationalist commitment it bears the hallmarks of that special black-world spirituality which

Baraka draws from the black nationalist Ron Karenga and which, as we have seen, dominates the essays of *Kawaida Studies*. In fact this collection of poems is dedicated to "advocates of Kawaida," and a significant proportion of it is actually a collection of prose homilies based on the teachings of Karenga. The collection also emphasizes the standard black nationalist fare of Baraka's writings at this period— the contrast between the old racial perversions and the new black pride, Africa as symbol of a universal "black" sensibility, and the philosophical ideal of social and individual wholeness. And as is true of Baraka's other black nationalist collections, *In Our Terribleness* suffers from the familiar weaknesses that seem endemic to his black nationalism—a philosophy of "blackness" that is too often little more than a shrill abusiveness of (black and white) antagonists, political claims that are sometimes mere bombast or facile revolutionism, and the questionable tendency, already noted in *Kawaida Studies*, of defining black American culture in exclusively urban terms.

But despite these familiar flaws *In Our Terribleness* does have merit. The highly deliberate process of rejecting white American culture in favor of "black" values has had the effect of intensifying the poet's interest in language itself as a symptom of cultural values and social conflict. Hence the redefinition of "magic" in *Black Magic*, from a limited, pejorative term in Western, technological culture is succeeded here by similar redefinitions. "Terribleness" is no longer a negative term. It is a synonym for goodness and beauty, for the positive qualities which Baraka is attributing to a new black self-awareness. In reversing the standard (white American) definition of the term Baraka intensifies the collection's pervasive sense of detachment from mainstream American culture. This self-conscious use of language is therefore integral to Baraka's political viewpoint in the poetry. And it is, simultaneously, a symptom of his continuing absorption in the role of style and form—in the very idea of art as both design and political process.

Accordingly, the pragmatic emphasis on the nuts and bolts of (black) nation-building proceeds here side by side with an intense awareness of art itself as a process of creating forms. The work of black artists like John Coltrane, Sun Ra, and Claude McKay is analogous to the imaginative creation of a vital black community. But black art is also more than an analogy. It is intrinsic to the process of sociopolitical creation because both processes, the artistic and the political, are inspired by ethnic pride and draw upon a sense of black cultural tradition. The poet's call for the building of new things in "Prayer for

Saving" is ambiguous, addressed to political worker and artist alike: "build new/ black beautiful things. New Shapes Buildings." [7]

There is a comparable self-consciousness, about the artist's creative use of language and style, in the subtitle of the collection: "Some Elements and Meaning in Style." "Style" refers both to culture (life-style, social values) and to the manner in which the artist's techniques or forms reflect that cultural "style." "Meaning" signifies the thematic or expressive role of the artist's style. "Elements" suggests the intrinsic values of black cultural "style" that are to be reflected in the artist's "meaning." And, finally, this deliberate blend of meanings has the crucial effect of defining art as cultural expression and as form with its peculiar or inherent "elements."

On the whole this kind of artistic self-consciousness lends itself readily to a certain innovativeness in matters of style and form, the kind of innovativeness that is drawing Baraka's poetry, in this collection, beyond the boundaries of the previous collections. The interweaving of poetry and essays, for example, remains on a tentative, somewhat experimental, basis in *Black Magic* where we find one major essay ("Gatsby's Theory of Aesthetics"). But *In Our Terribleness* takes this process a step further until the reader is left with what is not so much a collection of poems in the conventional sense but a continuous flow of words. And the flow varies from essay format to poetic images and back again. Moreover this continuous movement from one form to another confirms one of the opening phrases that describe the work as "a long image study in motion."

Altogether the form of the work takes the shape of a design that seems calculated to challenge rigid notions of poetic style or structure. This challenge is not unique to *In Our Terribleness* and has already been noted in the previous poetry. But the details of the challenge are more varied here, ranging from the absence of page numbers, the interweaving of essays and poems, to the lack of subdivisions and (in many instances) titles. Moreover Baraka's own reference to the work as "a long image story" pinpoints the effect of another feature. The collection relies heavily on images, the kind of verbal images that Baraka has cultivated since his early poetry and prose fiction. But in addition to those familiar images Baraka now depends on the visual images of the camera. The work is not only a collage of verbal or literary images. It is also a tapestry in which the verbal images of the poet are interwoven with the visual images of the photographer (Bill Abernathy).

Camera and words therefore combine to produce images that are

literally those of sight and sound. As a result verbal images often flow
from and reinforce photographic images. The picture of a black man
with a toothpick in his mouth gives rise to two distinct but integrated
images. In visual terms the white toothpick becomes a shaft of light
against a dark background. And in the verbal context of the poet's
imagination the transfiguration of the toothpick is taken a step further: the toothpick becomes a magic wand, an emblem of the man's
vital ethnic presence:

> The touch of light
> Transformed wood. A Wand. Transmutation. . . .
> His mouth wand.
> The toothpick of the blood is his casual swagger stick. . .
> Catches the light
> in the steel town
> catches a dancer's
> eye.

Finally, the process of interpreting the social significance of the
camera's images emphasizes the imaginative nature of the poet's own
perception.

This approach is sometimes unsuccessful, primarily because
Baraka's own revolutionary "swagger" leads to some questionable
interpretations of the camera's image. For example, it would seem
obvious enough that the photograph of a black youth holding an open
switch blade is a painful reminder of violence in the black community
where blacks are more frequently than not the victims of other blacks.
On this basis alone there seems to be nothing in the picture to justify
Baraka's rather questionable taste in rhapsodizing about the young
man as a symbol of revolution. Other failures are less distasteful and
result from Baraka's occasional tendency to strain for an effect. Hence
the photograph of an old man and a boy, one looking to the right and
the other to the left, is not the convincing image of a universal life
cycle that Baraka tries to offer us—even though this attempt involves
the poet's pervasive sense of wholeness, or "allness."

But in spite of such limitations these dual images of the camera and
the poetic imagination remain crucial to some understanding of
Baraka's perception of his art in *In Our Terribleness*. In relying as
heavily as he does here on the visual image Baraka is really taking to
its logical conclusion his continuing skepticism about the sufficiency
of words in ideal (that is, committed) literary art. Hence the relation-

ship between photographic image and poetic "word" here is actually a reciprocal one. The poet's imaginative vision adds new dimensions to the images captured by the photographer's imagination. Conversely, the camera's eye adds further conviction to Baraka's belief that language is inherently limited on its own, either as a tool for political change or as a means of communicating the complex and multiple images of the imagination. And in relying as much as he does here on non-verbal images to complete his poetic forms Baraka is once again using the sense of artistic structure to reinforce a political statement. In this case he is actually reinforcing the contention which recurs throughout *In Our Terribleness* that political creativity depends on much more than words, that political rhetoric must be integrated with the actions of political organization.

In both the political and aesthetic senses, then, the camera and the poetic imagination complete each other. And this impression of completeness is as crucial here as it always is in Baraka's work. The mutual dependency and the reciprocity of art forms (photography and poetry) attest to Baraka's continuing fascination with the distinctive province of the arts in general, and with the distinctive modes of each art form. But, equally important, when Baraka demonstrates the interdependence of such art forms and when he integrates their diverse images into one design as he frequently does in this collection he is also illustrating one of the recurrent themes of *In Our Terribleness*—that there should be a sense of wholeness in existence in general and in a reconstructed black "nation" in particular.

Both in its distinctive forms and in the reciprocity of those forms art is therefore a mirror image, reflecting the world as it is as well as prevailing visions of an ideal world. Hence in commenting on the photograph of a man gazing directly at the camera the poet exhorts, "Look into our eyes. Look into yr own eyes. . . . Can you see your own image?" The exhortation emphasizes the complex nature of art itself and its relationship with its human subject. The camera literally captures the man's image and therefore enables the subject to perceive himself in the art of the photographer. In this regard the photographer's art is graphically representative of art in general. To look into the images that constitute an art form is to see a reflection of oneself and one's condition. But this reflection is not merely a passive mirror image. It is also an active, creative process, one that completes the beholder's self-awareness in a way that is unique to the formal "elements" and social "meanings" of art. Hence in extending the "meaning" of the photographic image the poet's verbal image is really

a microcosm of that larger process whereby art in general completes
personal images of self.

Art is therefore not only a symptom of the Baraka ideal of wholeness, by virtue of interdependent forms. It is also the means whereby
the poet achieves a sense of wholeness, because its special images
enhance or enlarge our experience and perceptions. Art mirrors life,
returns the resulting images to us, and in turn our grasp of those
images completes our sense of self and experience in a special way.
The entire process duplicates the cycle of creation itself:

> There are mostly portraits here. Portraits of life. Of life
> being lived. Black People inspire us. Send life into us. . .
> We wanted to conjure with Black Life to recreate
>   it for ourselves. So that the
> connection with you would be a bigger Self. . . .
> The artist completing the cycle recreating.

On this basis the artist is a godhead of sorts, one whose role as
creator/recreator makes him the voice of both god the creator and
creation itself. And at this point Baraka's perception of his art merges
with his political interest in the black American's African past, for the
perception of the artist as the god's voice is comparable with the
traditional role of art in some traditional African cultures—the Akan
culture of West Africa, for example. In Baraka's words:

> The Creator has all experiences
> and we live as flying images of
> endless imagination. Listen to the creator
> speak in me now. Listen, these words
> are part of God's thing. I am a
> vessel, or black priest interpreting
> the present and future for my people.

Once again the emphasis is a double one. Baraka's insistence on the
representational, committed role of art goes hand in hand with his
continuing recognition of art as "images" of an "endless imagination."
Art is a microcosm of the process by which humans—blacks in this
instance—change and recreate their lives. And, simultaneously, it is
the special product of the imagination.

This definition of the artist as creator and as the godhead's voice
reappears in "All in the Street," one of the longer poems in *Spirit*

Reach (1972). The repetition is appropriate because it is fairly representative of the air of redundancy that pervades this volume. The themes are all repetitions, without the benefit of innovative variations, of the major black nationalist themes which Baraka explores in *Black Magic* and *In Our Terribleness*. In this regard *In Our Terribleness* suffers from a problem that insures that an earlier collection, *It's Nation Time* (1970), is merely a negligible rehashing of previous themes. *Spirit Reach* is at least salvagable on the basis of those few poems which, without being innovative, reiterate the familiar themes with a certain forcefulness. Hence the theme of spirituality relies heavily on the chant in "The Spirit of Creation Is Blackness":

> we merge with it
> all things are it
> we rhythm and sound and suncolor
> we rise and set and sing and move
> oh lord, oh lord, oh lord. . . .[8]

In one sense the reliance on the familiar and the repetitive suggests a certain flagging of imaginative energies. And this failing is amply demonstrated by the all but complete reliance on ideological clichés in the subsequent collection, *Hard Facts*. But the implications of this repetitiveness are not all negative. The heavy reliance on poetry as ritual chant in *Spirit Reach*, while representing a backward step from the experiments with multiple forms in *In Our Terribleness*, is also the reaffirmation of Baraka's major interest in language itself as a possible form of action—instead of being simply a prelude to or substitute for action. The chant is an actual process of inspiring and celebrating political change. As a collective activity it is a real example of Baraka's ideal of ethnic, communal, and cosmic unity.

Accordingly, the chant is both word and ritual drama, combining the direct exhortations and images of the word with a sense of that collective activism which is traditionally involved in the group chant. On this basis it is not difficult to see that the reiterated preference for the chant in his poetry reflects a certain restiveness with poetry itself as a useful vehicle for a politically active writer like Baraka. And at this point we can sense that he is less inclined to pursue the complex possibilities represented by the better poetry of *Black Magic* and *In Our Terribleness*. He seems more inclined to concentrate on ritual drama as his preferred form of committed art. In light of this it is significant that since the early 1970s Baraka's more significant publications have been in drama. This is the genre in which he has continuously remained active. This preference is appropriate since drama is peculiarly suited to his activist perception of art as both image and political action.

CHAPTER 6

Drama

I *The Word and the Act*

IN a recent essay on his plays Baraka poses and answers a question
that is fundamental to his writings and political activism as a
whole: "Is the Act as Legitimate as the Word? (A Question that could
only be asked in a bourgeois society, it is so absurd.) Now we know
that the act is *more* legitimate, it is principal!" Baraka's statement, his
most explicit on the tension between art and activism, is part of some
generalizations that he offers on the role of the artist from the perspectives of "Marxist-Leninist Mao Tse-Tung Thought." The emphasis on the greater legitimacy of the act over the word must therefore
be understood in relation to the Maoist insistence on the unity of
politics and art, on the fusion of "revolutionary political content" and
"the highest possible perfection of artistic form." Art that lacks "artistic quality" lacks force, even if it is politically progressive; and
although a poster or slogan may be politically valid, it lacks artistic
power (pp. 12, 14).[1]

In light of Baraka's development as a writer it is not surprising that
he is strongly attracted to the Maoist criteria which he quotes here
with approval. Here in the scientific socialism of "Marxism-
Leninism" and in Mao Tse-Tung's writings he finds a theoretical
framework for those aesthetic values which have always been inherent in the lifelong tension between artistic form and political commitment in his work. It is also appropriate that Baraka should
expound these values in the introduction to his most recent collection
of plays. First, the introductory essay itself and two of the plays (*The
Motion of History* and *S-1*) constitute some of his most detailed
statements on politics and art from a socialist perspective. The insistence on the unity of art and politics within that perspective is
particularly significant here because it is yet another example of the
manner in which Baraka's political attitudes remain consistent at the

135

most fundamental level, despite his movement from one ideological group to another. Hence the aesthetics of scientific socialism are comparable with those of the young radical rebel of the early 1960s and are really indistinguishable from some of the black aesthetic criteria of the late 1960s and early 1970s.

Second, the socialist ideal is peculiarly attractive to Baraka the dramatist, or more specifically, to Baraka the revolutionary dramatist. As a genre in which the distinction between word and act is blurred, drama is the means of achieving that unity of political action and literary word which has always been crucial to Baraka. Hence that interest in the word *as* act which dominates much of the later poetry culminates in the drama—especially in the later plays. In these plays the dramatic synthesis of language and action is both the symbolic and literal example of Baraka's ideal of the word as action. Indeed in Baraka's drama, even in the earlier works but especially in the more recent revolutionary plays, the very idea of dramatic form is both an aesthetic principle and a political concept: the play as action is integral to the revolutionist's idealistic activism; dramatic form as motion through time and space is compatible with the revolutionary view of history as constant change.

But curiously enough, although his theory of dramatic art is so integral to his political principles and practice, Baraka's achievement as a dramatist is decidedly uneven. Indeed, on the basis of those very socialist standards which he himself invokes, Baraka is least effective as a dramatist in the later revolutionary plays of his black nationalist and socialist periods. In one sense Baraka's insistence on the greater legitimacy of the act, as opposed to the word, does conform with the socialist ideal when "act" is understood as dramatic action: that is, the play itself is an activity that combines the formal action of dramatic art with the activism of a political ideal. And in this light it is understandable that the drama would increasingly become Baraka's preferred medium in recent years.

But in another sense the distinction between act and word seems to be carried, in practice, to the point where Baraka actually fails to live up to his socialist or Maoist ideal of art. His dramatic practice often leaves the impression that "act" should be understood simply as political action, rather than as dramatic action that combines artistic form with political content. On the one hand Baraka the artist obviously approves of the Maoist insistence on the unity of artistic form and political idealism. But on the other hand Baraka the political activist finds it increasingly difficult to maintain that unity in dramatic practice. On the whole we can still detect in his work, even at this stage, the familiar interplay between social commitment and a sense of the special nature of artistic form. But increasingly that balanced tension between the artistic and the political has slackened. As a result some works are little more than ideological statements by the politico who perceives his plays simply as a political act—as a political slogan or poster. As we have noted earlier, the politico's choice of an art form—the drama in this instance—as a political medium always involves a deliberate and crucial distinction between political statement and political art, at least in theory. And it would therefore be erroneous to ignore that implied or explicit distinction even when we are dealing with Baraka's baldest and least imaginative plays. But notwithstanding all of this it is clear that Baraka the political advocate has made it increasingly difficult for Baraka the dramatist to maintain an effectively balanced approach to drama as commitment and artistic design. And his later plays have progressively suffered as a result.

In chronicling his development as a dramatist Baraka's introduction to *The Motion of History* ignores his early plays, produced or published between 1963 and 1965. This omission is not surprising, in light of Baraka's disparaging references, in his preface to *Black Magic*, to his early poetry. More often than not Amiri Baraka has little patience with, or admiration for, the works of the nonrevolutionary LeRoi Jones. Moreover, the early plays tend to concentrate on the exploration of social contradictions and individual paralysis; but this exploratory approach is not likely to appeal to the revolutionist Baraka in view of his preference for drama that emphasizes symbolically decisive and transforming action. Yet on the whole it is reasonable to suggest that Baraka's own revolutionary aesthetic—the synthesis of political commitment and artistic design—is much closer to being realized in these early works than in his subsequent, more explicitly revolutionary, plays.

Of course from Baraka's current socialist perspective the nature of the political commitment is not altogether admirable in these four plays—*The Baptism, The Toilet, Dutchman*, and *The Slave*. These are not plays of revolutionary advocacy—not even *The Slave*, as we shall see in due course. Instead each work is a highly effective analysis of American society from a viewpoint that has not yet clarified itself beyond a passionate but ideologically vague radicalism. But notwithstanding that vagueness the commitment to the need for social change dominates each play. And at the same time this sense of commitment is integrated with Baraka's dramatic form with much more consistency than he is able to achieve in subsequent years.

Those later years fall into his black nationalist and socialist periods. From 1965 to 1972 Baraka wrote several plays on black revolutionary themes—including *Experimental Death Unit #1*, *Black Mass*, *Great Goodness of Life*, *Madheart*, *Arm Yourself or Harm Yourself*, *Police*, *Home on the Range*, *Slave Ship*, *The Death of Malcolm X*, *Jello*, *Junkies Are Full of SHHH. . .*, *Bloodrites*, *Ba-Ra-Ka*, and *Black Power Chant*. As Baraka himself has indicated, the actual list of works is longer if one includes the plays that were written but never produced or published, or others that were produced but not published (*MH*, 12–13). Viewed in the light of Baraka's revolutionary aesthetic the productions of these years are more distinguished by quantity than by quality. Many are ephemeral agit-prop pieces rather than substantial, committed theater; and they are more interesting as symptoms of Baraka's ideological perception of theater than as examples of substantial dramatic art.

Finally, since 1975 the plays, especially *The Motion of History* and *S-1*, have reflected Baraka's conversion to scientific socialism. On the whole this period reflects a significant shift in the playwright's perception of the nature of drama itself. The action and language of the black nationalist works tend to reflect the psychic and physical violence of racial violence; and in reflecting that violence the plays are implicitly, sometimes explicitly, offered as a means of galvanizing the black community into political awareness and action. But in the more recent socialist drama, like Brecht's, for example, the emphasis on the play as a teaching device is much more pronounced. In effect the play is not simply an ideological tool. By virtue of its role and actual themes it is an example of the scientific socialism that it espouses. Hence the function of the play as teaching device is underscored by the tendency to include characters who lecture others on the past (the motion of history) and on the ideals of scientific socialism. Consequently, although the complex design of the early plays will not be found in this more recent drama, we can still detect a continuing interest in the relationship between political content and the idea of design.

II   *The Early Plays*

The Baptism, first produced in 1964, is a useful introduction to Baraka's drama because it includes features that dominate the earlier plays and others that foreshadow subsequent developments in Baraka's dramatic art. Set in a church, the play is actually a modern morality drama about a young boy who is accused by an old woman of masturbating while pretending to pray. As the action unfolds it centers on a growing contest for the soul—and body—of the boy. The contest pits the old woman and the minister of the church against a homosexual who is contemptuous of his opponents' hypocrisy toward sex and who expresses a frank need for love and for an honest sexuality. The minister and the old woman are revolting not simply because they are puritanical but because their puritanism is a thin disguise for sexual desires (for the boy in this case) that they are unable to express frankly. As the contest becomes violent they strike the homosexual to the ground and in turn they are cut down by the boy who now claims to be the Son of God. At this point the play ends abruptly: the boy is carried off by a motorcyclist who is supposed to be a "messenger" of the boy's father.

As a morality play centered on a moral struggle between love and puritanism *The Baptism* exploits an old dramatic tradition with special ironic effects. The usual conflict between good and evil in the morality play tradition of Christian culture appears here with significant modifications. The forces of evil are now associated with the Christian Church itself; love and charity are embodied by the homosexual, a conventional figure of moral and sexual "perversion." And given the ambiguous figure of the boy himself (child figure and Christ archetype) then the moral struggle takes on an ironically twofold meaning: it is traditional insofar as it involves a contest for the soul of the human individual; and it is antitraditional in that Christianity is no longer an unquestioned symbol of goodness but is actually associated with evil. Indeed the most crucial outcome of the play's moral conflict is the degree to which Christianity emerges as an inherently corrupting tradition which makes it impossible for the individual to experience love and sexuality to the fullest, except on nonconformist or rebellious terms. Social traditions in the play are inherently destructive because they sanction a pervasive lovelessness and a neurotic fear of sex and feeling. The church is the main target in this regard because it is the institution which embodies these traditions.

The morality design of the play is, therefore, basically ironic in conception. Baraka recalls the old morality traditions of early Christian drama in order to attack those traditions and the Christian ethic that they espoused. And insofar as *The Baptism* subverts Christian morality and art, it anticipates the use of the morality play format in

Baraka's black nationalist, anti-Western drama. For in those later plays, as we shall see, political conflicts take on the form of moral contests in which a Western dramatic tradition (the morality play) becomes a device for rejecting the West itself. Moreover, this subversive, antitraditionalist use of tradition is reflected in the play's title. The ritual of baptism is no longer an initiation into the established conventions of religious belief and social morality. It has now become a ritual of exposure and subversion, one directed against the conventions themselves.

Similarly the ritual of religious sacrifice acquires a new significance in the play. The minister and the old woman insist that the boy must be "sacrificed" in order to atone for his sexual "sin." But their demand is really a hypocritical evasion. The choice of the boy as sacrificial victim allows them to evade the consequences of their destructive attitudes towards sexuality. It enables them to divert attention from the repressed sexual longings that are so manifest in their "moral" rhetoric—especially in the old woman's suggestively detailed account of the boy's sin: "You spilled your seed while pretending to talk to God. I saw you. That quick short stroke. And it was so soft before, and you made it grow in your hand. I watched it stiffen, and your lips move and those short hard moves with it straining in your fingers for flesh. . . . Your wet sticky hand. I watched you smell it." [2]

In effect the planned sacrifice allows them to avoid the sinfulness of their own hypocrisy and the emotional destructiveness of their puritanism by treating "sinfulness" as a problem that can be solved through the ritual sacrifice—of another. Indeed the very idea of ritual, whether of baptism or sacrifice, is associated in the play with elaborate systems of hypocrisy and self-evasion. Hence Baraka's adaptation of such rituals for the form of his play amounts to the ironic use of ritual as a form of protest and rebellion—against established rituals (systems) and their associated social values. And here too *The Baptism* anticipates Baraka's black nationalist drama where the idea of ritual and the forms of established ritual are associated with the culture that is being rejected by the play.

Both as morality play and as ritual drama *The Baptism* is distinguished by a marked emphasis on the idea of role playing. The characters have no names as such. They are presented as types (old woman, minister, homosexual, boy and messenger); and as such they are social roles reflecting the cultural values that are central to the play's themes. In this instance each character's personality reflects a theatrical self-consciousness about her or his role: the minister is the sanctimonious voice of Christianity; the old woman energetically acts out her identity as the symbol of female chastity; the homosexual deliberately exaggerates his role as a "queen" in order to emphasize his calculated contempt for social convention; and the boy moves self-consciously from being the familiar symbol of childhood innocence to being a Christ-child.

On the whole this pointed presentation of characters as roles has the effect of emphasizing the degree to which the conventions and values attacked in the play have encouraged individuals to assume roles that reflect social norms instead of giving free play to honest feeling. In this sense the stereotypical nature of such roles is a form of social realism, for it underscores the limiting and deforming effects of established traditions on the human personality. This, too, explains the significance of self-conscious role playing in the other plays. In each instance the issue of roles reflects the dramatist's careful integration of his theme with his sense of dramatic art: the role playing of dramatic theater is also a symptom of social reality.

Altogether, then, *The Baptism* is an impressive example of Baraka's early ability to synthesize dramatic form and theme. And this synthesis is linked with the play's major theme—the failure of love in contemporary society. The very issue of forms, roles, and rituals is crucial in the play because they have become empty shells in the absence of any real feeling. Consequently moral statements and declarations of love are invariably hypocritical, particularly when they are made by self-consciously traditional figures. The role of the homosexual is therefore particularly ironic in this regard: the alleged pervert emerges as the healthiest of the lot because he frankly expresses his commitment to love and because he refuses to accept the puritan antithesis between flesh and spirit. He is the subversive outsider, pitted against the minister who is the loveless, and unlovable, apostle of Christian "love" and "charity." The homosexual's candor about love and sex (he does not disguise his erotic interest in the boy) amounts to a virtue. On the other hand the minister and the old woman attempt to disguise their love for the boy with the rhetoric of puritan morality. In so doing they corrupt their sexual response to the boy. Their puritanism has transformed it into mere prurience. As in *Preface to a Twenty Volume Suicide Note* puritan hypocrisy has turned love into an evil thing. This kind of transformation is also the burden of the later, black nationalist plays where white racism and black self-hatred are linked to the general fear of love in society. It also dominates the theme of an early work like *The Toilet*, where, as in *The Baptism*, the general failure of love is thrown into sharp relief by the role of the homosexual as subversive outsider.

Originally produced in 1964, *The Toilet* is set in an urban high-school toilet. The plot is rudimentary. Ray Foots leads a group of boys in crude horseplay which rapidly culminates in violence. The victim of the violence is Karolis, a sensitive boy who is accused of having written a love letter to Foots. Karolis surprises Foots by refusing to deny the accusation and by insisting on fighting him. Discomfited by Karolis's honesty and belligerence Foots tries to avoid the fight on the ground that Karolis has already been badly beaten by members of the gang. But Karolis persists, beats Foots, who has to be rescued by the other boys, and is battered into unconsciousness by the gang. Karolis is left lying on the toilet floor, but after a brief interval Foots sneaks back in tears to cradle Karolis's head in his arms.

The toilet setting remains throughout the play as its dominant symbol. Its appearance and smells suggest the ugliness and filth that Baraka attributes to his characters' social and moral milieu. In turn this vision of America as toilet defines the personalities of the characters themselves. The choice of toilet as setting shrewdly duplicates the usual adolescent preference for the toilet as the stage for a certain kind of brutish bravado or for covert rebelliousness. In individual terms the filth and stench represent the unsavory personalities of Foots and his gang. Finally the privacy of the toilet lends itself to the theme of repression—the repression of love—which runs throughout the play.

The moral corruption that is suggested by the toilet setting is associated here with a kind of perverted masculinity. Foots and his gang represent a cult of manhood which takes the form of mere brutishness. This brutishness is reflected in the inane but violent dialogue and by an intense, neurotic need to dominate others in verbal jousting or in improvised forms of boxing and basketball. In turn this corrupted maleness is attributed to the failure of love in Foots's world. As in *The Baptism* the theme of moral and emotional corruption is heightened by a sense of irony. In this instance the irony is centered on the name "Love" borne by a member of Foots's gang. And as in *The Baptism* this irony is intensified by the fact that it is the alleged pervert, the homosexual, who emerges as the most humane of these young males going through the traditional rites of passage into manhood.

Karolis's humanism and heroism consist of the fact that he has the kind of courage which enables him to express his love in the incriminating letter and to affirm that love in the face of hostility. Ironically, the sleazy privacy of the toilet has become the setting for a certain kind of public declaration or self-revelation, one that strikes at the guilty secrecy with which society perceives love and with which Foots eventually responds to love. By a similar token the conventionally "masculine" hero, Foots, emerges as an antihero: he is contemptible in his fearful need to deny and punish Karolis's love, and is pathetic, at best, in that final moment of his belated, and secret, demonstration of love.

Finally, that secrecy ends the play on a note of unequivocal realism. It confirms the continuation of these prevailing social codes which encourage a guilty secrecy about sex and emotional experience. The toilet setting therefore remains crucially significant to the very end. It defines the filthiness that results from the denial of feeling in Foots and his kind. Foots's declaration of love at the end is actually corrupted by the social values which dictate secrecy; and the toilet symbolizes the persistent corruptions which result from those values. The play's setting is therefore a dynamic force in the action of the play and in the experience of the characters. And on this basis it reflects a rather impressive grasp of theater as the total integration of setting, action and character.

Dutchman, first produced and published in 1964, also reflects a rather self-conscious use of setting. Here the setting is a subway, "heaped," according to the playwright, "in modern myth." [3] The subway is less intimately involved in the personalities and action of the play than is the toilet in *The Toilet*. In *Dutchman* the setting owes its significance to the manner in which it evokes mythic materials that are, in turn, interwoven with the play's themes and action. The winner of the Obie award for the best off-Broadway production of 1964, *Dutchman* has perhaps been the most widely discussed of Baraka's plays; and this popularity is attributable, in part, to the interest of critics in the role of myth in the play. [4]

In examining *Dutchman* as mythic drama it is important to take seriously Baraka's description of the setting as one that is "heaped" in myths. Any approach that singles out one mythic theme will miss the degree to which the play's structure depends in part on the interweaving of several myths. The underground setting recalls the holds of the slave ships, and this image is reinforced by the title itself: the first African slaves were reportedly brought to the New World by Dutch slave traders. The image of slavery is further reinforced by the possibility that the underground setting refers to the famous "under-

ground railway" which assisted runaway slaves on their way from the
South to the North. The Dutch reference may also be linked with the
legend of the Flying Dutchman—the story of a ship doomed to sail
the seas forever without hope of gaining land. This ship is also
supposed to be a slave-trading vessel.[5] In turn the theme of retribu-
tion in the legend of the Flying Dutchman links the idea of a curse
with the history of slavery. Slavery insured the loss of American
innocence quite early in American history. That is, it undermined the
American's claim to some special kind of functional idealism. And
here the complex formation of images and myths include biblical
myth, for like the descendants of Adam and Eve after the biblical fall,
contemporary Americans must cope with the consequences of a prior
curse—in this instance the curse of slavery.

Finally, Adam and Eve have their counterparts in the play. The
black Clay (Adam) and the white Lula (Eve) are both linked by
America's fearful fascination with the sexual juxtaposition of the black
man and the white woman. Clay is the black American Adam,
tempted by the forbidden fruit of Lula's white sexuality. On her side,
Lula's sexual fascination with his blackness is interwoven with her
racial condescension toward him. The play's plot revolves around the
ethnosexual implications of Baraka's handling of myths. As a white
American Lula is both the forbidden sexual fruit and the Flying
Dutchman, compelled by the curse of racism and historical slavery,
to engage in a series of repetitive actions that reflect the recurrent
guilt, fascination, and hatred with which whites view blacks in the
society. Hence she boards the subway train, engages Clay in conversation (on race and sex), then stabs him to death when his initial
attraction changes to scornful resentment at her racial condescension. And after Clay's body has been removed she prepares to engage
another young black man who has just boarded the train.

The total effect of the play's mythic structure is twofold. It creates
the impression of continuity in the issues with which the myths are
associated—racial oppression, destructive sexual attitudes, and an
emotionally paralyzing puritanism. But the structure also heightens
our awareness of the characters as social types. Notwithstanding
Baraka's well-known disclaimer (Home, 187), Lula and Clay are not
simply unique individuals. They are clearly archetypal figures representing social traditions (racial and sexual) and exemplifying the
behavior that results from those traditions. Lula, for example, is at
pains to emphasize that she is a type; and she feels old because as a
type she represents generations of attitudes. She also perceives Clay

as a type whose personality seems quite open to her because he belongs to a well-known pattern.

Lula and Clay are both types in this sense. And at the beginning of the play they are clearly presented, on the basis of their interaction, as racial and sexual stereotypes—Lula the white goddess and white liberal, and Clay the naively middle-class black stud. This stereotypical dimension is a calculated aspect rather than mere defect of the play. It arises from the perception and behavior of the characters who have chosen to limit their humanity within the confines of racial and sexual stereotypes that have been molded by social conventions. They are deliberately acting out predetermined roles instead of attempting to comprehend and communicate with each other's humanity. The built-in element of theater operates at a conscious level in the play. Hence Lula elaborates upon her self-description as a type by remarking that she is an actress, and Clay suggests that their encounter has proceeded as if it had been written as a script. As in *The Baptism* role playing is not simply a theatrical device; it is also deliberately chosen pattern of social behavior. The protagonists' choice of stereotypical roles is a symptom of their limitations; and in turn, the roles which they choose are intrinsic to the dramatic structure of the play itself.[6]

Moreover they are presented and judged on their acceptance of these roles, and on their ability to look beyond the pretence in their own roles and in the roles of the other. Lula is very conscious of her role as the white goddess of America's racial mythology and chooses to revel in the destructiveness of that role. By a similar token she is incapable of dealing with Clay when he ceases to be an Uncle Tom and a black stud. Her white indifference to the humanity of blacks and to the essence of their culture is epitomized by her shallow interpretation of the blues as mere "belly-rub" music. On his side Clay fails initially, insofar as he accepts Lula's stereotypical attitudes and insofar as he caters to those attitudes by being the black stud and Uncle Tom. This failure proves fatal in the long run because it allows Lula to establish the kind of interaction that leads to his death: having subordinated himself to her sexual fantasies and her liberal condescension, he inevitably drives her to destructive anger by asserting his humanity.

However, Clay's failure is not complete. He gains a limited triumph in that very assertion of humanity which makes his death inevitable. At first he shifts from the bland, self-effacing acquiescence of the Uncle Tom to the covert hostility which allows him to agree, sarcastically, when Lula assumes that black history and black music evolved out of big happy plantations in the slave-holding South. This covert hostility is soon replaced by open resentment. He castigates Lula's one-dimensional image of blacks and mocks her inability to realize that in many instances the blacks who seem to conform with this image are really rejecting her by subversively acting out her fantasies. They are playing roles based on "lies."

Clay's own interpretation of the blues reflects his own growth from mere role playing to a complex rebel: the blues are not mere "belly-rub" music but the expression of complex experiences ranging from joy and sorrow to despair and rage. As Clay interprets the blues he himself grows into a complex humanity and away from the racial and sexual perspectives of Lula and her "type." In the process we discover in his character the same kind of rebelliousness that he attributes to the blues tradition. Lula destroys Clay the rebel because his rebellion threatens her by destroying the stereotypes and myths that are essential to her own sexual and racial roles.

Yet Clay also fails in the end because, although his rebellious perspectives are substantial enough, his identity as a rebel is incomplete. Even as he expounds on the power and integrity of black music, Clay unfavorably compares himself with the musician as ethnic artist. Clay himself is a poet whose art lacks, in his opinion, the ethnic integrity of black, grass-roots forms like the blues: as a derivative of Western literature his own writings are a "kind of bastard literature," and his poetry is an escape from direct rebellious action. His words as poet have become a contemptible substitute for the act: "Safe with my words, and no deaths, and clean, hard thoughts, urging me to new conquests" (p. 35).

Clay's bitter self-analysis is based on two familiar and recurrent themes in Baraka's work. As a black writer and intellectual Clay is caught up in a cultural conflict which paralyzes him, limiting his capacity for rebellious action, despite his intellectual awareness of the need for rebellion. On the one hand he is drawn to Lula's ethnocentric white culture, but on the other hand he responds to the black ethnicity represented by the blues. His death, therefore, represents the self-destructive consequences of this kind of moral and intellectual paralysis. Second, Clay's ineffectuality as rebel stems in part from the fact that his poetic art is self-contained rather than actively committed to social action. His is literary art for art's sake. He suffers from a fascination with words for their own sake. As Clay himself admits, blacks "don't need all those words" (p. 36). On this basis it is

easy to see the close connections between the theme of rebellion in
Dutchman and the advocacy of change in the more explicitly revolutionary plays of a later period. Given Clay's limitations, the issues of
rebellion and change are curtailed in this play. Here the question is
not one of advocating change as such. This is to come in the later
plays. In *Dutchman* we are offered an analysis of those things which
make rebellion and change little more than imagined possibilities in
the lives of Clay and his "type," but which will become urgent options
when the idea of rebellion combines word and act.

Despite its setting—a revolutionary race war—*The Slave* is closer
to *Dutchman* than to the later revolutionary plays in that here, too,
we have a work that analyzes the potential rebel. The subject of
analysis in this case is Walker Vessels, the leader of the blacks in the
race war. The action centers on his encounter with his former wife,
Grace Easley, and her present husband, Bradford (both white), when
he returns to Grace's home at the height of the fighting. It is a violent
encounter that is marked by racial recriminations on both sides, and
the sounds of the race war outside provide the background for this
personal conflict. The confrontation ends with the house collapsing
under shell fire. Grace dies just after realizing that her two children
by Walker are dead, either as the result of Walker's war or directly by
his hands.

It is easy enough to see the play, on its literal level, simply as
another black militant fantasy of racial revenge. But such an approach
does not really do justice to the more complex and interesting features of the work. Here, as in *Dutchman*, the play's conflicts center
on the tensions within the black protagonist. Although the play's
action emphasizes the desirability of radical change, it is actually
more significant as an extended analysis of those attitudes which
stimulate or retard the capacity for radical ethnic change within the
black psyche. In this regard we should view Grace and Bradford not
simply as representatives of the white world around Walker but also
as embodiments of his white, Western perspectives, those perspectives which inhibit his racial pride by encouraging self-hatred. As a
poet, for example, Walker feels that his art has been compromised by
a certain dependency on the Western tradition. Hence the white
Easley is expected to recognize Walker's poetry and literary tastes
because they both share the same intellectuality. Walker hates Easley as the white enemy outside, but he loathes and fears him as the
symbol of the "whiteness" within himself.

Grace is comparable with Bradford Easley in this respect. She is

the image of that white femininity that has historically attracted a
certain kind of self-hating black male. Thus Walker's previous marriage to her represents a self-destructive obsession. It is an obsession
that has formed the racial triangle of black man, white woman, and
white man—even in Shakespeare. As Walker muses aloud to his two
antagonists, "Remember when I used to play a second-rate Othello? . . . You remember that, don't you, Professor No-Dick? You
remember when I used to walk around wondering what that fair sister
was thinking? . . . I was Othello . . . Grace there was Desde-
mona . . . and you were Iago" (p. 57).

In short, the black imitation of whites is represented by the Iago-
Easley figure of teachery—teachery to one's racial identity. And the
self-destruction that is inherent in that treachery is embodied by the
half-man (Professor No-Dick) whose alleged impotence represents
Walker's crippled humanity as a black. In reviling Grace and man-
handling Easley during their confrontation Walker tries to exorcise
his crippling white self-perception. The contrast in the play between
the strong, masterful black Walker and the weak white Easley has
little to do with Baraka's alleged "endorsement of the stereotype of
Negro sexuality." [7] It represents, instead, an internal conflict—within Walker—between an assertive racial integrity and the stunted
awareness that results from the denial of one's black identity.

Easley, then, personifies the cultural values and racial attitudes
that compromise Walker's role as revolutionary. This point is implicit
in the title. Having progressed from the status of a slave in the
prologue (where he addresses the audience in the guise of a field
slave), Walker is going through a transitional stage in which he now
recognizes his continuing intellectual serfdom as it is incarnated in
Easley, his cultural alter ego. The "race war" of the plot is, therefore,
less important as a literal happening than it is significant as an
allegorical background for the conflicts within Walker. Indeed the
manner in which Baraka presents Walker at the beginning and conclusion of the play emphasizes the allegorical nature of the race war.
The physical violence and the emotional confrontations in the play
are actually a projection of Walker's subjective experience as a split
personality. And in keeping with that subjective context, these
events assume a dreamlike form if they are viewed in relation to the
words of Walker Vessels when he appears in the prologue as an old
field slave: "We know, even before these shapes are realized, that
these worlds, these depths or heights we fly to smoothly, as in a

dream, or slighter, when we stare dumbly into space, leaning our eyes just behind a last quick moving bird, then sometimes the place and twist of what we are will push and sting, and what the crust of our stance has become will ring in our ears and shatter that piece of our eyes that is never closed" (p. 43).

Walker is actually preparing his audience for a "dream," a self-revealing vision that will disturb and awaken. And since this is to be a form of self-revelation then it will shatter that apathy ("stupid longing not to know") which characterizes the slave mentality. The shattering of this apathy can create "killers" (real revolutionaries) or "foot-dragging celebrities," who exploit their "militant" image for personal gain (pp. 43–44). Applied to the events that follow the prologue Walker's remarks imply that the race war incidents and the confrontation with Grace and Bradford Easley are the elements of a vision that reveals Walker's divided ethnic consciousness to himself and to the audience. That consciousness includes a capacity for revolution, for the radical reshaping of his ethnic perception.

In this connection, Walker's physical relationship with the main action of the play strongly suggests that the latter is a kind of dream sequence: he is an old man in the prologue, and at the end of the introductory speech he "assumes the position he will have when the play starts" (p. 45). If this physical transformation (from old field slave to Walker Vessels) suggests that there is a "fading in" to the main-action dream sequence, then the physical change at the end of the play is equally suggestive: as Walker the rebel leader stumbles out, he becomes "the old man at the beginning of the play" (p. 88)—signifying the "fading out" of the dream.

All of this brings up the question of Walker's actual identity. He himself points to his ambiguity in the prologue: "I am much older than I look . . . or maybe much younger. Whatever I am or seem . . . to you, then let that rest. But figure, still, that you might not be right" (p. 44). He is warning against a literal approach to his character, for he is really an archetype of the black experience. He is therefore both older and younger than he looks because he incorporates the past and the present; and his dream opens up future possibilities. The "old" field-slave personality is the key to this archetypal role. That role is ambiguous. In one sense his servile status symbolizes the subjection to white images and cultural values. But in another sense his identity as a *field* slave points up rebellious potential. In this latter regard he recalls Malcolm X's interpretation of the field slave's image in black history. Unlike the "house Negro" who loved the white slave-master, the "field Negroes" hated the master and were always eager to rebel or run away from slavery.[8]

Malcolm X's field Negro and Baraka's field slave are the same archetype. He is characterized by a predisposition toward rebellion. And as such an archetype Walker represents both past and present ("older" and "younger") militancy. To return to the words of the prologue Walker's ideas involve the rediscovery of a long history of black militancy and resistance: "Old, old blues people moaning in their sleep, singing, man, oh, nigger, nigger, you still here, as hard as nails, and takin' no shit from nobody" (p. 45). Walker's consciousness of black dreams of rebellion and his interest in the blues as a tradition of resistance confirm his own rebellious predisposition. And in turn that predisposition lends itself to dreams of revolution—the kind of dream that constitutes the main action of the play.

Walker's capacity to dream of revolution in specific terms and his growing sense of commitment take him beyond Clay's rather muddled impulses in *Dutchman*. But in general Walker is comparable with Clay in that he too suffers from a destructive split-consciousness. As in Clay's case this division stems from the unresolved tensions between his identity as a militant black and his continuing involvement with (white) cultural norms that inhibit his militant potential. And like Clay, Walker is hamstrung by a frustrating dichotomy between word and action. Hence his failure as a poet is not only caused by a self-hating imitation of white models. His poetry has also failed because it exists apart from his dreams of revolutionary change. The (literary) word and (revolutionary) action remain separate in his character. Hence whether it is considered as a literal event or, more interestingly as Walker's fantasy, the race war remains an inchoate happening rather than a concrete action informed by a shaping revolutionary imagination.

III   *Black Revolutionary Drama*

Baraka's involvement in the black nationalist movement stimulates a significant shift in his drama. In his black revolutionary plays theater is no longer a process of reenacting or analyzing tensions, or conflicts, between the revolutionary idea or word and the political act. It attempts, instead, to be an example of the dramatic art as political action. That is, theater itself is a political activity by virtue of the fact that the play has become a form of political advocacy. But although the theater of political advocacy would seem to fulfill Baraka's ideological ideals—as black aesthetician and later as scientific socialist—the plays of this period seldom meet the criteria which he himself admires in Maoist aesthetics. Many of the plays are ideologically "correct," from Baraka's black nationalist viewpoint, but they seldom approximate that "highest possible perfection of artistic form" which Baraka is later to demand of political art (*MH*, 14).

A basic problem, one that is seldom resolved in this period, is that Baraka finds it difficult to use drama for sociopolitical purposes while maintaining convincing dramatic forms. Consequently, too, many of the plays are little more than the kind of bombast that appears in the preface to his *Four Black Revolutionary Plays*: "We are building publishing houses, and newspapers, and armies, and factories/ we will change the world before your eyes." [9]

A. *Short Pieces*

Many of the plays of this period are little more than agit prop. As we have already noted, several of these remain unpublished; and on the basis of these shorter pieces it appears that Baraka is not often interested in the play's dramatic design. At other times potentially interesting dramatic forms (street theater and ritual drama, for example) lack thematic substance. Some works are mainly polemics against white racism. *Home on the Range* (1968), for example, depicts members of a white suburban family through the eyes of a black burglar. They appear as a collection of dim-wits who talk gibberish. *The Death of Malcolm X* (1969) dramatizes the events leading up to Malcolm X's assassination as a white conspiracy involving brainwashed blacks. But the more interesting plays are less concerned with white society as such and are more involved with examining the black experience itself from a black nationalist point of view.

Experimental Death Unit #1 (1965) belongs to this latter group. It depicts a street scene during an apparent black revolt. A patrol of black soldiers encounters a black prostitute and her two white customers and kills all three. The symbolism is obvious enough. Prostitution represents the broader historical experience in which blacks barter their humanity in order to be accepted or merely tolerated by white society (*Four Black Revolutionary Plays*, 1–15).

The title of *Arm Yourself or Harm Yourself* (1967) sums up the simple message: blacks who hesitate to arm themselves against violent whites (particularly the police) are choosing suicide. The suicidal nature of nonviolence is, therefore, emphasized by the death of three brothers at the hands of the police—as they stand on the street debating the merits of armed militancy versus nonviolence.

Police (1968) is partly based on pantomime. It centers on the dilemma of a black police officer whose job places him in the role of killing blacks on behalf of whites. He is hated by those whites, and he is despised by the blacks who eventually drive him to suicide during a riot. The police officer's life symbolizes the split loyalties which afflict many blacks. His death becomes the black community's symbolic ritual of expunging self-hatred and racial treachery. Significantly, the self-hatred that destroys the police officer is associated with older blacks. The young blacks are the revolutionaries. They drive the police officer to suicide, and at the end of the play they promise to return in order to take care of "some heavy business." The events of the play spark the promise of fundamental changes that are associated with a new (young) consciousness.

Black youth also spearhead the revolution in *Junkies Are Full of SHHH. . .* (1971). Here Damu and Chuma set out to rid the community (Newark) of drug pushers. In the process they kill the whites who control the drug traffic, and Bigtime, the principal black drug pusher. The play concludes with Bigtime's body being pulled out to be displayed on the street as a message to the community.

These plays are all linked by the fact that they are street theater. Their setting is primarily or exclusively the streets of black neighborhoods. Their themes are rooted in the "street" experience (prostitution, police actions, rioting, and drug traffic). And they are obviously aimed at those people whose lives are influenced by these street experiences. Moreover, as the rather grisly ending of *Junkies* demonstrates, street theater of this kind treats the street as a kind of medium, a communications device that may be used destructively (by junkies) or constructively (by young revolutionaries spreading their message). Consequently, the very idea of street theater exploits the familiar image of the street itself as a living dramatic environment, an environment that offers its audience a variety of messages. The play's setting defines its scope and action.

In addition to the theater of the street, Baraka also produced a number of other short pieces which are really based on ritualistic pantomime, dance, and chant. These are the plays of the later black nationalist period in which the emphasis is on the celebration of blackness rather than on exorcising white racism or black self-hatred. In this vein *Bloodrites* (1971) is a ritual dance. It features groups of blacks dancing around (white) devil figures and chanting black power slogans in Swahili. The devils wither away in exhaustion while the blacks gain increasing strength from their dance and chants. *Black Power Chant* (1972) is precisely what its title signifies: a group of dancers chant black power slogans as they move about on the stage. *Ba-Ra-Ka*, too, is based on song, dance, and political slogans.

On the basis of theme these plays are undistinguished. They never move beyond the obvious. The really interesting feature of such plays lies in their design and impact as spectacle. Dance (act) and chant (word) are integrated within highly stylized forms of ritual. And despite the intellectual thinness of these works they represent Baraka's continuing interest in ritual as drama, an interest that has obviously grown from the satiric subversiveness of *The Baptism* to the use of ritual as a legitimate medium in its own right. Here it is the medium of celebration, drawing upon the rhetoric of black power slogans, as well as the rhythms of black dance and music. In the process this kind of theater is intrinsically bound up with the experience that it celebrates: it is a an expression of black power—a symptom of the movement rather than simply an enactment of it.

B. *The Longer Plays*

Despite their obvious flaws Baraka's short plays are generally more interesting than most of his black nationalist dramas. These shorter works provide some direct clues to Baraka's dramatic imagination in terms of street theater, ritual drama, and theater as a committed art form. And as such they offer the audience a relatively more stimulating experience of theater than much of what Baraka has produced since the first major plays. The longer black nationalist pieces, however, reflect no significant innovations in Baraka's dramatic writing, although their themes are more ambitious than those of the shorter works.

Black Mass (1966), a science fantasy in the Frankenstein tradition, is typical of the limited achievement of the longer plays. As the title indicates, this is another example of Baraka's ritual drama. In this case the ritual is based on the religious myth, "Yacub's History," in the Nation of Islam (previously known as the Black Muslims).[10] Here the idea and function of ritual are closer to the satiric themes of *The Baptism* than they are to the themes of celebration in the short black nationalist plays. The title is therefore ironic: it confirms the evil connotations of black mass (black magic) and black identity in white,

Christian culture; but at the same time it defines evil on an anti-Christian, antiwhite basis. Hence the evil in the play is really caused by a black scientist, Jacoub, who creates the first white being, a creature that quickly turns out to be a monster. The beast corrupts and destroys blacks—including Jacoub himself—by tainting them with its whiteness.

The beast represents Jacoub's moral bankruptcy and his racial self-betrayal. In creating the beast Jacoub panders to what the black nationalist perceives as a sterile need to create for the sake of creation. Jacoub does not envisage his creation in any functional sense. And on this basis his scientific talent belongs to that tradition of a narrow, self-serving rationalism which Baraka repeatedly attacks in his writings. But Jacoub's scientific narrowness is not only suspect on this moral basis. It is also reprehensible because it reflects his racial self-hatred. Creating for the sake of creating, whether in art or in science, is a "white" Western value system, and in catering to such a value system Jacoub betrays his racial and cultural tradition—a functional tradition, as defined in black nationalist terms. Thus the cries of the white beast ("White! . . . White! . . . Me . . . Me . . .") reflect Jacoub's self-destructiveness. Although the cries express the racist's megalomania in one sense, they also express that racial self-deprecation which has historically eroded black pride and cultural values. As Jacoub's fellow scientists warn him, his undertaking negates human feeling and decency and represents "the emptiness of godlessness," because it involves the betrayal of his ethnic and moral integrity (p. 25).[11]

The moral and ethnic implications of Jacoub's personality are also linked with Baraka's perception of time and history. Jacoub's invention involves the "discovery" of time; but, as his colleagues protest, time is merely a demon that turns human beings into "running animals" (pp. 22–23). Jacoub's obsession with time is therefore suspect because it implies the subordination of the human personality to the rigid categories (exemplified here by time) of a narrow, rationalistic view of experience. And in ethnic terms this obsession is another symptom of Jacoub's racial self-hatred: his rationalism is clearly identical to that scientifically defined concept of time and history which Baraka repeatedly attributes to white, Western culture, and which associates "progress" and the very idea of human "development" with clock time.

Finally, the play contrasts Jacoub's rationalism with a more integrated and complex perception of science—science as complete knowledge encompassing reason, spirit and feeling, rather than as a narrow technology dedicated to the creation of systems for their own sake. The "compassionless abstractions" that Jacoub's colleagues deplore in him are therefore "anti-life" because they represent the "substitution of thought" for feeling (pp. 26, 34). At this point Baraka's familiar redefinition of magic, especially black magic ("black mass"), is crucial. The "true" scientists (Jacoub's colleagues) are magicians in that here, as in the *Black Magic* poems, magic represents knowledge as an integrated and creative process. On the other hand, Jacoub's fragmented approach to science as an enclosed system is destructive. His is a limited kind of knowledge in that it is divorced from humanistic concerns and moral values. This kind of science is a perverted and destructive kind of "magic," and Baraka ironically invests it with all the negative connotations with which white, technological cultures have responded to nonwhite traditions of "science." That is, he is now treating Jacoub's "white" science as evil magic, as a form of "witchcraft" or "superstition." The very idea of black magic therefore emerges from the play as an ironically ambiguous concept. It connotes (a) the black nationalist ideal of a creatively integrated approach to knowledge and experience, and (b) the evil magic which Western culture and blacks like Jacoub develop from a limited approach to science—at the same time that they reject the nonwhite ideal of knowledge as mere "superstition" and "black magic."

On the whole the themes of *Black Mass* are full of complex possibilities. But the play is badly flawed. Quite apart from the theatrically unconvincing plot and the self-defeating shrillness, Baraka fails to exploit fully the idea of ritual that his title so deliberately invokes. The play's ambitious complex of themes therefore remain unlinked with the kind of formal, ritualistic design that is promised by the work's title and religious background.

Great Goodness of Life, subtitled "A Coon Show," is one of Baraka's better black nationalist plays. While *Black Mass* harks back, unsuccessfully, to the satiric use of ritual form in *The Baptism*, *Great Goodness of Life* continues Baraka's earlier interest in the theater's role playing as a symptom of social roles. The idea of the "coon show" is therefore bound up with the play's presentation of racial types. Blacks and whites are satirically presented as stereotypes which they have imposed upon themselves as well as upon others. The racial role playing of society is actually an extended coon show in which white racism fosters a sense of superiority by attributing the subhuman coon role to blacks. And in their turn blacks reinforce their inferior status by playing this attributed role. The coon in this show is Court Royal; and the setting, a courtroom, heightens the impression of a "show" or piece of theater by virtue of the dramatic nature of judicial proceedings.

Court Royal has been accused by the white court of having harbored a murderer. He knows nothing about the crime with which he is charged, but as a racially timid and conservative black he is easily intimidated into accepting the court's final edict: he must expiate his "crime" by shooting the murderer, and as a result his soul will be "washed white as snow" (p. 62). Court Royal complies with the edict, then celebrates his freedom and "white" soul without once reacting to the fact that the young "murderer" claims him as father in the moment of death. As the play ends Court Royal suddenly assumes a lively pose and announces to Louise (off-stage) that he is going to the bowling alley for a while.

That closing vignette contrasts with the opening scene which is set outside an old log cabin, presumably in a rural setting that is far removed from the urban environment of a bowling alley. The shifts in time and place are comparable with similar changes in *The Slave*. The juxtaposition of past and present, black rural roots and black urban present, dramatizes the continuity and the pervasiveness of the destructive attitudes represented by the coon show. And as in *Dutchman* these continuities are reflected in the play's deliberate emphasis on social types and role playing: by their very nature the stereotypes of the coon show underscore the enduring nature of the racial attitudes that they embody.

In his other major black nationalist play Baraka returns once again to a dramatic form that he first utilizes in his early drama. *Madheart* (1966) is subtitled "A Morality Play," and it therefore recalls the morality play tradition upon which *The Baptism* draws. In *Madheart* the "moral" conflicts of the morality drama are defined in terms of black nationalism. They center on an ethnosexual battle for the black male's soul, or more precisely, for his sexual allegiance. At the same time these conflicts involve a struggle for the racial integrity of the black everywoman who is torn between the old desire to imitate white models of femininity and the new black insistence on racial pride and black beauty.

The ethical and ethnic struggles of the play's themes are developed within an unconvincingly melodramatic plot. Black Man and Black Woman vanquish the seductive arrogance of the (white) Devil Lady.

Then they undertake, in the spirit of black unity, to "take care" of the sick ones—Mother and Sister—who are still fascinated with white standards of sexual beauty. On the whole the moral tensions of the play are linked with the black male's consciousness and personality. He feels compelled to destroy the "whiteness" of Sister's self-hating images of white femininity, not only for her own sake, but for his own: he needs to eradicate from within himself his destructive obsession with the white woman as a supposedly superior being. He is both repelled by and fascinated with the white woman (Devil Lady) for these reasons. And this fascination-abhorrence is emphasized by the scene in which he destroys Devil Lady. The manner of the execution is both a form of revenge and a kind of self-betrayal: he thrusts arrows, a spear and a stake into her genitals, thereby tainting the act of execution with the suggestive connotations of rape.

In this connection it is significant that Devil Lady is presented as a masked figure. The white mask suggests not only a white presence as such but a white image imposed upon and accepted as a sexual norm by black men and women. And in this latter sense the "execution" of Devil Lady is really an act of self-cleansing by the black man and his ally, Black Woman. In turn this cleansing has implications that go beyond the immediate sexual issue. The Devil Lady image represents white culture at large as it is interpreted from a black nationalist viewpoint—a culture in which moral and social values, as well as goods, are marketed through the media by the exploitation of the (white) woman's sexual image. In the inelegant language of Baraka's Devil Lady, "My pussy rules the world through newspapers. My pussy radiates the great heat" (p. 70).

The sexual issues that Baraka explores here are not essentially innovative insofar as they are related to the black experience. But in linking these issues with the broader social context as well as with the racial theme, he offers a potentially complex and interesting viewpoint of his subject. Despite that potential, however, *Madheart* is unconvincing at best and more often than not is offensive and bombastic. The main problem stems from the dramatist's sexual perceptions, especially his perception of female sexuality and female roles in society. On one level, for example, it is possible to justify the manner in which Black Man executes Devil Lady by indicating that this reflects his lingering fascination with the white woman's sexuality even in the very moment at which he attempts to expunge the myth of white (sexual) superiority from his consciousness. But on another level, it is difficult to escape the conclusion that this kind of crude genital violence reflects a deeper, disturbing response to female sexuality as such, irrespective of race. It is the kind of response in which the ideal woman is the subjugated woman and in which the most attractive form of female sexuality is one that is accessible, for whatever reason, to a neurotically masculine need to engage in repetitive rites of phallic domination.

In effect the rather shrill themes of ethnic regeneration amount to little more than a thinly disguised rehashing of certain male preconceptions that Baraka, black nationalism notwithstanding, shares with nonblack men. Black Man's disposal of Devil Lady bears all the hallmarks of old, universal traditions of masculine dominance. So does Black Man's relationship with Black Woman. From a certain point of view that relationship is no more satisfactory than the ethnosexual order of things that it is supposed to replace. Both the "new" black man and the "new" black woman have disposed of their sexual and racial self-loathing in order to reaffirm all the traditional values of masculine superiority and feminine submissiveness. He therefore demonstrates his need for her by slapping her, and his new sense of "manhood" depends upon her submission to him and to her defined role as mother: " 'I want you, woman, as a woman. Go down' (*He slaps her again*.) 'Go down, submit, . . . to love . . . and to man, now, forever.' " She assures him of this newly found "strength" by submitting to his strength—and his sperm: "I am your woman, and you are the strongest of God. Fill me with your seed" (pp. 81, 83).

The sexual ideal that Baraka espouses here is also advocated in his political essays. Indeed *Kawaida Studies* reflects his personal confusion and distress at the possibility that the conventions of female subordination may be replaced by new sexual roles bases on equality. The black woman, he insists, is the black man's "divine complement." As for sexual equality, "We do not believe in 'equality' of men and women. We cannot understand what devils and the devilishly influenced mean when they say equality for women. We could never be equals . . . nature has not provided thus" (p. 24). And according to this natural scheme of things the black woman must inspire her man and teach the children. Curiously enough it does not strike Baraka the black nationalist that a political ideology which demands equality for blacks while denying equality to women is self-contradictory. And this contradiction severely limits the scope and depth of *Madheart*.

On the whole *Black Mass*, *Great Goodness of Life*, and *Madheart* are centered primarily on attacks upon white society and white attitudes among blacks. And Baraka develops these attacks in a generally less interesting way than the manner in which he handles themes of ethnic growth and celebration in the other major plays of his black nationalist period—*Jello* and *Slave Ship*. *Jello* was written in the middle 1960s and was originally scheduled to be published with the other works that eventually appeared in *Four Black Revolutionary Plays* in 1969. But the publisher balked and the play finally appeared separately in 1970. It is a satiric parody of "The Jack Benny Show," featuring all the main characters of the original television show—Jack Benny, his black valet Rochester, Dennis, Mary, and the announcer Don Wilson.

In *Jello* Rochester is no longer the surly but basically compliant servant. He is now a black militant who stages his own rebellion by refusing to work for Benny. He quits his job after robbing Benny and the others. The effectiveness of the play depends in part on its close parody of the original show. Baraka captures the style and personalities of the Jack Benny program. Indeed the play self-consciously underscores this similarity: hence Rochester is able to "rebel" with relative ease because for much of the proceedings his antagonists assume that his actions are all part of "The Jack Benny Show" itself, that the entire incident is just a joke.

In turn this leads to another aspect of the play's effectiveness. The well-developed scenes in which Rochester's victims believe that this is all in fun have a twofold effect. They dramatize the degree to which "reality" and "fantasy" are blurred in Rochester's world. White fantasies about blacks are part of a social reality in which the "good" black is the docile Uncle Tom (the old Rochester) and in which the idea of black militancy is something of a joke. And, ironically, such fantasies make it difficult for whites to recognize the validity of militant claims when blacks do break away from the docile stereotype. Moreover, the banal fantasies of television, including programs like "The Jack Benny Show," are mirrors of that general insipidity which Baraka consistently attributes to American culture at large. In this regard *Jello* is comparable with *Home on the Range*, where the gibberish of the white suburban family is presented as an echo of television. Finally, the realism of the play allows the audience to perceive convincing links between Rochester, the new militant, and Rochester, the old Uncle Tom. Despite his compliance the original Rochester is sufficiently saucy in his relationship with Jack Benny to suggest a certain predisposition toward rebelliousness. And Baraka's militant really brings out into the open the rebelliousness that seems to lurk under the surface of the Uncle Tom image.

As in *The Slave* the militant's violence implies a previous, long-standing potential for revolt. Unlike *The Slave*, however, *Jello* is a literal statement in the sense that Rochester is no mere dreamer of revolutions, as Walker Vessels is. Rochester's actions are not invested with those ambiguities which confirm the suspicion, in *The Slave*, that the race war is an imaginary event taking place in Walker's fantasies. Indeed in *Jello* there is a sustained emphasis on the contrast between (white) fantasies and (black) action. Consequently Rochester is an unreal or imaginary rebel only when he is perceived through eyes that can see him only as Benny's lackey, as the comically irreverent but fundamentally docile Uncle Tom. Thus while the play gradually strips away Benny's white liberalism to expose the racism with which he views Rochester, it simultaneously forces whites to awaken slowly from their racial fantasies and to see Rochester's personality and actions as they really are. In effect the play seeks to confront whites with what is really happening, notwithstanding deeply rooted needs to ignore or distort the realities behind black militancy.

Despite Rochester's personal success in forcing the recognition of his actions and new attitudes, *Jello* as a whole avoids that facile wish-fulfillment which too often mars Baraka's black nationalist writings. Thus although Rochester escapes with the stolen money and compels his victims to recognize him as he is, his triumph is counterbalanced by the continuity of the social order against which he is rebelling. Thus before he is knocked out and robbed by Rochester, Jack Benny's announcer (Don Wilson) assures the television audience that "The Jack Benny Show" will return as usual the following week. The announcement amounts to an assurance of continuity—the persistence of white fantasies even after the revelation of black attitudes. Indeed the play as a whole is a wry tribute to the power of the media, especially television, in reinforcing and perpetuating entrenched viewpoints in white America: Rochester's individual rebellion, like the actual revolts of the 1960s, has become a television "event," recognizable as an actual experience with disturbing implications for the white audience but easily transformed into an entertaining spectacle that leaves old fantasies untouched after the initial moment of disturbance. Hence the play as a whole balances the celebration of a black revolutionary idealism against the persistence of certain social attitudes in white America. But, paradoxically, the intransigence of white attitudes actually heightens the importance of Rochester's rebellion by underscoring the need for black modes of perception that arise from a new black awareness instead of depending upon the old, and continuing, white indifference. This blend of revolutionary idealism and social realism is rare in Baraka's black nationalist writings, and it is largely responsible for the success of *Jello* as a complex drama and entertaining theater.

Slave Ship, (1967), "a historical pageant," is one of Baraka's more successful experiments in ritual drama. The plot is minimal. It consists of images, dances, and pantomime together with sporadic dialogue; all is designed to dramatize the physical and psychic experiences of slavery from the holds of the slave ships to contemporary American society. The play's real strength lies in the audiovisual impact of its materials. Much of the action takes place in darkness or half-light. This suggests the hold of a slave ship, and the relative lack of lighting accentuates the variety of sounds upon which Baraka builds his themes and his dramatic effect—African drums, humming of the slaves, cries of children and their mothers, shouts of slave drivers, and cracking sounds of the slaver master's whip.

The succession of audiovisual forms is integral to the pattern of ritual upon which Baraka bases his historical pageant. The sights and sounds of the slave ship remain throughout, but they alternate from time to time with other forms which depict successive stages of black American history—the plantation of the slaveholder, the nonviolent civil rights movement, and the black nationalist movement. History itself becomes a succession of rituals, particularly the ritual of suffering which gives way after repeated cycles to the new rituals of racial assertion and cultural awakening. The music which dominates the play is integral to the ritualistic pageantry of history. At first the main sounds are those of the African drum, accentuating the fresh African memories of the new slaves. Then as the plot moves toward the contemporary period the sounds of the African drum are gradually integrated with the musical forms that evolved in black American history since slavery. And this musical progression culminates in the blues and jazz idioms both as forms of protest and as the celebration of black nationalism. By a similar token the humming of the slaves in the holds of the slave ships gradually gives way to the sounds of protest and eventual triumph.

But throughout all of this the audience is always in touch with the persistent sounds and sights of the slave ship itself, for this is the setting that remains for the duration of the play, and the subsequent historical epochs are actually superimposed upon it in sequence. The historical pageant is, therefore, both progressive in direction (moving from slavery to the black nationalism of the 1970s) and circular (reinforcing a sense of the moral and social continuities of the society: the slavery of the past exerts a powerful influence on the circumstances of the present). Moreover, the persistence of the slave ship images has the effect of defining history itself as movements (progressive and cyclical) through time. Similarly the ritualistic forms of the play (dance, chant, and pantomime) are each a microcosm of the historical process: each synthesizes the materials inherited from a previous generation with the experiences of the contemporary period. And by extension this kind of synthesis characterizes the play as a whole. As a pageant that combines past and present experiences, traditional forms and new materials, it reenacts the historical process as Baraka defines it.

IV   Socialist Drama

Slave Ship predates Baraka's major socialist dramas by several years. But the play's historical themes, and historically defined structure, make it a direct forerunner of *The Motion of History* (1976) and *S-1* (1976). And this remains true despite the fact that *Slave Ship* is not committed to socialist ideology. The perception of history in all three plays is intrinsic to Baraka's emphasis on the theater as a teaching device. In black nationalist drama like *Slave Ship* the reenactment of history fulfills a major assumption of black nationalism: the full understanding of black history is crucial to a vital sense of black identity because the crippling of black pride in the past has been partly the result of white distortions of black history. Moreover, the very process of reenactment becomes a form of celebration, the celebration of that black ethnicity which emerges from the exploration of the past.

On the whole this approach to the play as teaching device and as celebration is similar to the fundamental premise of Baraka's socialist drama, although in the latter there is a far more explicit self-consciousness about the teaching role. The norms of "scientific socialism" reflect a certain commitment to education: the inevitability of the socialist revolution is partly the consequence of politically enlightening the masses. Art, especially dramatic art, facilitates the revolutionizing process by depicting the past and its impact on the present. While the black nationalist's historical sense enhances the discovery and celebration of a distinctive black culture, the historical perspectives of scientific socialism encourage the social awareness that will hasten revolution across racial lines. As Baraka himself describes *The Motion of History* and *S-1*, "both plays are vehicles for a simple message, viz., the only solution to our problems . . . is revolution! And that revolution is inevitable. *The Motion of History* brings it back through the years, focusing principally on the conscious separation created between black and white workers who are both exploited by the same enemy" (*MH*, 13).

Both plays also reflect a continuing weakness in Baraka's committed art. In this socialist phase, as in the black nationalist period, he suffers from a tendency to indulge in ideological wish-fulfillment at the expense of social realities. Hence the earlier habit of exaggerating the depth and breadth of black nationalism in America has been replaced by unconvincing images of one great socialist rebellion in all the countries of the world (*The Motion of History*) and by the highly unlikely spectacle of the American labor union movement as an anticapitalist, prorevolutionary force. Of course these "weaknesses" are less troublesome if we are inclined to accept the underlying purpose of such plays: they are concerned less with strict social realism as such, and more with the advocacy of social change.

The realities that invite "scientific" analysis in these plays are the facts of history, the kind of historical data that forms the plot of *The Motion of History*. The play is actually a series of historical vignettes. The first act depicts scenes from the early civil rights movement of the 1950s and 1960s in order to attack the futility and self-destructiveness of nonviolent protest. Thereafter the play interweaves the ethnic and labor union movements of the twentieth century with past rebellions. The earliest slave uprisings, the abolitionist movement, and the political conflicts of the Reconstruction period are all dramatized as responses to a repressive caste system that is based on class and economics rather than race. Racial conflicts that do occur are portrayed as the outcome of a deliberate policy, by the ruling elite, of stimulating racial divisiveness in order to prevent solidarity among the working classes.

Like *Slave Ship*, *The Motion of History* dramatizes the "motion" of history on two levels. The multiple historical episodes which form most of the play emphasize the cyclical nature of American history by presenting exploitation and rebellion as continuing features of the society. But the play's conclusion emphasizes a progressive movement toward the kind of radical change that will dispense with the traditional cycles of continuing repression and abortive rebellion. And by emphasizing history as a progressive force, the play's theme and structure dramatize the "inevitability" of socialist revolution as the culminating result of that progression.

S-1 is less heavily dependent on historical data than is *The Motion of History*. There are a limited number of scenes that depict examples of judicial and political repression in America's past. But on the whole the plot centers on a mythical incident that is historically significant because it is an extension of the old repressiveness and because it hastens the historical inevitability of revolutionary reaction among the masses. The thin plot centers on the passage of a law (S-1) that severely limits political activities and freedom of expression. Revolutionary groups organize resistance to the passage of the law, and after it comes into effect they plan widespread defiance of it. The play concludes on an optimistic note: the revolutionaries celebrate their unity and purpose (*MH*, 151–225). The play's real strength, and one of its few merits as theater, lies in Baraka's ability to integrate his dramatic form with the conflicts that constitute his political scenes.

In this regard S-1 achieves a limited success of the kind that *The Motion of History* never approaches. Thus Baraka is able to eke out some sense of the dramatic from the series of confrontations on which the play's plot is based. The judicial debates on the merits of the new law, in the Supreme Court, are enhanced by the inherently dramatic setting of the courtroom; and this setting is again exploited to effect in the trial of Red (one of the revolutionary leaders) on charges of treason. In a similar vein Congress provides the setting for another series of confrontations—the debates between "liberals" and "conservatives" about the law and the current social unrest. The dramatic experience centers here on the interaction of ideas. This is the theater of ideological positions rather than one of character and situation, and in this respect S-1 is the culmination of a trend that has been developing in Baraka's dramatic writings since his earlier black nationalist plays.

This kind of drama does have its built-in limitations, of course. The characters are rudimentary types conceived in very broad terms, so broad indeed that the revolutionary figures of S-1 are indistinguishable not only from each other but from their counterparts in *The Motion of History*. Scenes in which ideological conflicts are presented are severely underdeveloped, largely because the extreme sketchiness of the characterization limits the possibilities of the very confrontations that are supposed to dramatize the clash of ideas. And as a result of all this the audience is left with a theater of rhetoric in which potentially interesting situations and personalities are inundated with a flood of repetitive statements from all sides of the political landscape. Ironically enough Baraka's lack of emotional control in his ideological statements and his increasing indifference to characterization have resulted in a thin, one-dimensional drama that contravenes his own ideal of dramatic art as one that fuses word, act, and idea. Instead what he has produced is largely a loosely connected series of scenes filled with the shopworn clichés of reactionaries and revolutionaries alike. At its worst this method exemplifies the predominance of ideological word over dramatic art, the very kind of imbalance that Baraka himself abhors in theory. Curiously enough, at this stage of his career as dramatist his theory of effective drama is less compatible with the kind of plays that he prefers to write, and it is more appropriate to the early plays which he does not choose to mention in his introduction to *The Motion of History and other Plays*.

CHAPTER 7

Mirror of His Society

O N the whole the uneveness of Baraka's drama is fairly represen- tative of his general achievements as a writer. For even at its least distinguished his writing reflects a continuing tension between the decidedly unsubtle ideologue and the committed artist, between a passion for literal political statement and an interest in art as an imaginatively conceived, expressive, and committed design. And this tension remains in the background even when the interest in imaginative art is merely theoretical. Moreover, as the genre that spans his writing career his drama appropriately reflects a major constant in his writings. That is, despite his ideological shifts, his themes and their underlying social attitudes have remained fairly consistent.

Consequently, his perception of American society is invariably bleak. He always envisions a society of moral corruption and human decay whenever he contemplates America. This moral revulsion at America as a wasteland has a twofold effect. On the one hand it inspires those images of violence and death which characterize much of Baraka's work, ranging from the early radicalism and the black protests and moving to the later revolutionism of the black nationalist and socialist periods. And, on the other hand, this revulsion also triggers a passionate commitment to life, that is, to the moral and social rebirth which he envisages in his successive alternatives (ethnic, socialist, and so forth) to the American wasteland.

Moreover, the moral overview of America is always integrated with his racial themes. The black American's plight as racial victim is both a primary concern in its own right and an important symptom of America's pervasive ills. And this remains true even in the deliberate emphasis on nonracial criteria in the socialist drama where the issue of racial violence and divisiveness is emphasized as the sign of an exploitive and oppressive ruling elite. Racial anger and moral outrage have always been inextricably interwoven in Baraka's work. Consequently, the thematic complexity of his more substantial work has easily eluded critics, both hostile and sympathetic, who respond only to his ethnic militancy. Finally, it is necessary to recognize the degree to which the shock tactics of moral outrage really arise from the fact that Baraka is a familiar kind of moral idealist, one whose idealism motivates the wasteland images of the "Beat" poetry, the black revolutionism of the middle years, and the more recent themes of socialist revolution.

The underlying thematic continuities of Baraka's work are complemented by certain consistencies in his approach to certain forms or techniques. The images of sight and sound which he emphasizes as a narrative technique in his only novel and in his short stories go back to his earliest poetry. And at the same time these images are adapted to the requirements of the black nationalist poems where the sounds of political statement are indistinguishable from the forms of politically committed art. In the drama the morality play tradition and the interest in ritual forms continue from the earliest plays to the later revolutionary works.

The continuity of certain forms attests to a strong degree of artistic self-awareness in Baraka the writer. This is the kind of self-awareness that springs from his lifelong commitment to the integration of theme with artistic form, and even when that integration is more a matter of promise than practice it makes for a complex context in which to examine Baraka, one in which the reader must be constantly alert to the actual or possible relationship between form and content, rather than neglecting one in favor of the other. This is the major reason for the enormous demands that Baraka's work, even at its worst, places on the reader. At its worst the work suffers from a narrowness of vision and a shrillness of tone that frequently distort the effects of whatever structural achievements might exist. But his best writing is challenging in the other sense: the closely knit relationship between theme and form requires a painstaking attention to the manner as well as the substance of statement—a requirement that has often proven too difficult for those who are overly hostile toward or enthusiastic about the substance.

Finally, Baraka's achievement as a writer should also be weighed on the representative nature of his political activism and art. In fact his career as a whole can be seen as a political weather vane of sorts. The early period reflects that combination of concerns which influences much of American literature and politics in the late 1950s and early 1960s: there is a growing uneasiness about America's world role and the country's relationship with the Third World; and there is increasing recognition that the black civil rights movement raised questions about American society in general as well as about racial relationships. The middle period, the years of Baraka's black nationalism, coincides with the militancy of black America's black power movement and the racial riots in the cities. Finally even the more recent conversion to socialism is symptomatic, notwithstanding the fact that scientific socialism is not a popular movement in America at this time. His current ideology and writings are representative in that they reflect a general turning away from cultural nationalism and racial confrontation in black American politics since the early 1970s. Although Baraka denounces the "black petite bourgeoisie" who simply exploited black nationalism in order to feather their nests in the mainstream culture, Baraka's own switch to scientific socialism is as much an admission of the failure of black nationalism as is the opportunism that he condemns in the black middle class.

The decline of ethnic politics in black America reflects a marked decrease in political energies, a decrease that can be attributed to the opening of some doors to the mainstream and to the death, imprisonment, or discrediting of the political leaders of the 1960s. Baraka himself is a good example of this decline of political energies. As a scientific socialist he is in the least imaginative phase of his life as a political writer. This relative lack of creativity is not really the fault of the ideology itself. It seems, more likely, to be the reflection of a certain intellectual flabbiness on Baraka's part. Not only in the forgettable poems of *Hard Facts* but also in the plays and essays of the later years, Baraka seems to find it increasingly difficult to go beyond the accepted clichés of political dogma. It has appeared progressively easier for him to offer hackneyed and literal statements in lieu of artistic forms that are both imaginative and sociopolitically significant. Of course the current flabbiness is not necessarily terminal. In light of his career as a whole Baraka is unlikely to remain pedestrian as a political activist or mediocre as an artist. And whatever further developments occur in that career they will, in all likelihood, be closely linked with the literary and political atmosphere of his time. His significance as a mirror of his society has been one of his most enduring characteristics.

Notes and References

Preface

1. See, for example, Don M. Menchise, "LeRoi Jones and a Case of Shifting Identities," *College Language Association Journal* 20 (1976–1977): 232–34.

Chapter One

1. Theodore A Hudson, *From LeRoi Jones to Amiri Baraka* (Durham, N.C., 1973), pp. 9–10.
2. Ibid., p. 14.

Chapter Two

1. LeRoi Jones, *Home: Social Essays* (New York, 1966); page references in text.
2. Amiri Baraka, *Raise Race Rays Raze: Essays Since 1965* (New York, 1972); page references, identified by short title (*Raise*), in text.
3. *The Autobiography of Malcolm X* (New York, 1964), p. 268. Compare with Washington, *The Politics of God: The Future of the Black Churches* (Boston, 1967), pp. 3–4.
4. *Kawaida Studies: The New Nationalism* (Chicago, 1972); page references in the text, identified by *KS*.
5. Hollie I. West, "Karenga's Joke: A Merry Kwanzaa to All," *Los Angeles Times*, May 31, 1978, p. 1.
6. *Black World*, July 1975, pp. 30–42.
7. LeRoi Jones, *Black Music* (New York, 1968), pp. 11–20; page references in text.
8. One of the more representative collections of black aesthetic essays is *The Black Aesthetic*, ed. Addison Gayle, Jr. (New York, 1971).
9. For the "universalist" view see, for example, C. W. E. Bigsby, *Confrontation and Commitment: A Study of Contemporary American Drama* (Columbia, Missouri, 1967), pp. 115–16.
10. *Voices in the Whirlwind and other Essays* (New York, 1972), pp. 76–77.
11. Gayle, ed., p. xiii.

12. LeRoi Jones, *Blues People: Negro Music In White America* (New York, 1963), p. x.

13. *Shadow and Act* (New York, 1966), p. 250.

14. Recent studies of Baraka have traced this aspect of his aesthetic to his reading of Hegel (*Aesthetik*). See Kimberly W. Benston, *Baraka: The Renegade and the Mask* (New Haven, 1976), pp. 90–93.

15. LeRoi Jones, *Black Magic: Collected Poetry 1961–1967* (Indianapolis, 1969), pp. 116–17; further references in text.

Chapter Three

1. According to John O'Brien, Baraka's aesthetic is not simply antiwhite as such. It is anticolonial in its emphasis on the undesirable dominance of Europe in American culture and arts. See *Interviews with Black Writers* (New York, 1973), pp. vii–xi.

2. David Littlejohn, *Black on White: A Critical Survey of Writing by American Negroes* (New York, 1969), p. 96.

3. Edward Margolies, *Native Sons: A Critical Study of Twentieth-Century Negro American Authors* (Philadelphia, 1968), p. 198. Less hostile, more useful insights into the novel are offered by Kimberly Benston, *Baraka: The Renegade and the Mask* (New Haven, 1976), pp. 12–30; Esther M. Jackson, "LeRoi Jones (Imamu Amiri Baraka): Form and the Progression of Consciousness," *College Language Association Journal* 17 (September 1973): 33–56.

4. "Technique as Discovery," *Hudson Review* 1 (1948): 67–69.

5. LeRoi Jones, *The System of Dante's Hell* (New York, 1966); page references in text.

6. Edward Margolies, *Native Sons* (p. 198).

7. See James Baldwin, *The Fire Next Time* (New York, 1962), pp. 27–29.

8. *Selected Essays 1917–1932* (London, 1932), p. 14.

9. Erich Auerbach, "The Survival and Transformation of Dante's View of Reality," in *Dante: A Collection of Critical Essays*, ed. John Freccero (Englewood Cliffs, N.J., 1965), p. 12.

10. Compare Edmund L. Epstein, *The Ordeal of Stephen Dedalus: The Conflict of the Generations in James Joyce's "A Portrait of the Artist as a Young Man"* (Carbondale and Edwardsville, Ill., 1971), pp. 5–11.

11. See A. Walton Litz, *James Joyce* (New York, 1966), p. 78.

12. See, for example, Robert Bretall, ed., *A Kierkegaard Anthology* (Princeton, 1951), p. xxiv; Jean Wahl, "The Roots of Existentialism," in Jean-Paul Sartre, *Essays in Existentialism*, ed. Wade Baskin (Seacus, N.J., 1972), pp. 3–12; further references in the text.

13. Susan Sontag, "On Style," in *Against Interpretation and Other Essays*, (New York, 1969), p. 30; Schorer, "Technique as Discovery."

Chapter Four

1. LeRoi Jones, *Tales* (New York, 1967); page references appear in the text.

Chapter Five

1. Charles Olson has explained the tenets of the projective school in his *Human Universe and other Essays* (San Francisco, 1965), pp. 52–61.
2. LeRoi Jones, *Preface to a Twenty Volume Suicide Note* (New York, 1961); page references in text, identified by *Preface*.
3. See, for example, C. W. E. Bigsby, *Dada and Surrealism* (London, 1972), pp. 4–10.
4. "Imamu Amiri Baraka: The Quest for Moral Order," in *Modern Black Poets: A Collection of Critical Essays* (Englewood Cliffs, N.J., 1973), pp. 113–17.
5. *The American Adam: Innocence Tragedy and Tradition in the Nineteenth Century* (Chicago, 1955), pp. 5, 9; further references in text.
6. LeRoi Jones, *The Dead Lecturer* (New York, 1964); page references in text, identified by *Dead*.
7. Amiri Baraka, *In Our Terribleness: Some Elements and Meaning in Black Style* (Indianapolis, 1970), no page numbers.
8. Amiri Baraka, *Spirit Reach* (Newark, 1972), pp. 23–24.

Chapter Six

1. Amiri Baraka, "Introduction," *"The Motion of History" and other Plays* (New York, 1978); page references in text, identified by *MH*.
2. LeRoi Jones, *"The Baptism" & "The Toilet"* (New York, 1966), p. 16.
3. LeRoi Jones, *"Dutchman" and "The Slave"* (New York, 1964), p. 3.
4. Some of the more useful discussions of myth in *Dutchman* include George R. Adams, "Black Militant Drama," *American Imago* 28 (Summer 1972): 107–28; Kimberly W. Benston, *Baraka: The Renegade and the Mask*, p. 155; and Werner Sollors, *Amiri Baraka/LeRoi Jones: The Quest for a "Populist Modernism"* (New York, 1978), pp. 129–33.
5. Compare Sollors, *Amiri Baraka/LeRoi Jones*, pp. 130–31, and Sherley Anne Williams, *Give Birth to Brightness: A Thematic Study in Neo-Black Literature* (New York, 1972), pp. 106–107.
6. See Robert L. Tener, "Role Playing as a Dutchman," *Studies in Black Literature* 3 (Fall 1972): 17–21.
7. C. W. E. Bigsby, *Confrontation and Commitment: A Study of Contemporary American Drama 1959–1966* (Columbia, Missouri, 1967), p. 140.
8. Malcolm X., *Malcolm X Speaks* (New York, 1966), p. 11.

9. LeRoi Jones, *Four Black Revolutionary Plays* (Indianapolis, 1969), p. viii.

10. According to the Black Muslims (Nation of Islam) the white race evolved from an inferior being that was originally created by Yacub, a mad black scientist. A summary of the myth, "Yacub's History," appears in Malcolm X, *The Autobiography of Malcolm X* (New York, 1964), pp. 164–67.

11. *Four Black Revolutionary Plays* (Indianapolis, 1969); succeeding page references in text.

Selected Bibliography

PRIMARY SOURCES

1. Anthologies Edited

African Congress: A Documentary of the First Modern Pan-African Congress. New York: William Morrow, 1972.
Black Fire: An Anthology of Afro-American Writing. New York: William Morrow, 1968. Coedited with Larry Neal.
The Cricket: Black Music in Evolution. Newark: Jihad Productions, 1969.
Fidel Castro. New York: Totem Press, 1959.
Four Young Lady Poets. New York: Totem Press, 1961.
The Moderns: An Anthology of New Writing in America. New York: Corinth Books 1963.

2. Drama

Arm Yourself or Harm Yourself. Newark: Jihad Productions, 1967.
"The Baptism" & *"The Toilet."* New York: Grove Press, 1966.
Ba-Ra-Ka, in *Spontaneous Combustion: Eight New American Plays,* ed. Rochelle Owens. New York: Winter House, 1972, pp. 175–81.
Black Power Chant, in *Drama Review* 16 (December 1972): 53.
Bloodrites, in *Black Drama Anthology,* ed. Woodie King and Ron Milner. New York: New American Library, 1971, pp. 25–31.
The Death of Malcolm X, in *New Plays from the Black Theatre,* ed. Ed Bullins. New York: Bantam Books, 1969, pp. 1–20.
"Dutchman" and "The Slave." New York: William Morrow, 1964.
Four Black Revolutionary Plays. Indianapolis & New York: Bobbs-Merrill, 1969.
Home on the Range, in *Drama Review* 12: 4 (Summer 1968): 106–11.
Jello. Chicago: Third World Press, 1970.
Junkies Are Full of SHHH. . ., in *Black Drama Anthology,* ed. Woodie King and Ron Milner. New York: New American Library, 1971, pp. 11–23.
"The Motion of History" and Other Plays. New York: William Morrow, 1978.
Police, in *Drama Review* 12:4 (Summer 1968): 112–15.

3. Essays

Black Music. New York: William Morrow, 1967.
Blues People: Negro Music in White America. New York: William Morrow, 1963.
Home: Social Essays. New York: William Morrow, 1966.
Kawaida Studies: The New Nationalism. Chicago: Third World Press, 1972.
Raise Race Rays Raze. New York: Random House, 1971.
"Why I changed My Ideology: Black Nationalism and Socialist Revolution," *Black World* (July 1975), 30–42.

4. Poetry

Black Magic: Collected Poetry 1961–1967. Indianapolis & New York: Bobbs-Merrill, 1969.
The Dead Lecturer. New York: Grove Press, 1964.
Hard Facts. Newark: People's War, 1975.
In Our Terribleness: Some Elements and Meaning in Black Style. Indianapolis & New York: Bobbs-Merrill, 1970. With Bill Abernathy.
It's Nation Time. Chicago: Third World Press, 1970.
Preface to a Twenty Volume Suicide Note. New York: Totem Press, 1961.
Spirit Reach. Newark: Jihad Productions, 1972.

5. Prose Fiction

The System of Dante's Hell. New York: Grove Press, 1965; Evergreen Edition, 1966.
Tales. New York: Grove Press, 1967.

SECONDARY SOURCES

1. Bibliography

DACE, LETITIA. *LeRoi Jones: A Check List of Works by and about Him*. London: Methuen, 1971. Centers primarily on the works and studies of the 1960s.

2. Books

BENSTON, KIMBERLEY W. *Baraka: The Renegade and the Mask*. New Haven: Yale University Press, 1976. Evaluates contributions from black and Western sources to Baraka's philosphy and art. Includes bibliography.

HUDSON, THEODORE R. From *LeRoi Jones to Amiri Baraka*. Durham, N.C.: Duke University Press, 1973. The biographical sections are the real strength of this pioneering book-length study. Includes bibliography.

RICARD, ALAIN. *Theatre et Nationalisme: Wole Soyinka et LeRoi Jones*. Paris: Presence Africaine, 1972. A pioneering comparative study of Baraka and the Nigerian dramatist [French text].

SOLLORS, WERNER. *Amiri Baraka/LeRoi Jones: The Quest for a "Populist Modernism."* New York: Columbia University Press, 1978. Analyzes Baraka's work on the basis of the writer's sociopolitical themes and commitment. Includes bibliography.

3. Parts of Books and Articles

ADAMS, GEORGE R. "Black Militant Drama." *American Imago* 28 (Summer 1972): 107–28. Provides useful insights into the role of biblical myths in *Dutchman*.

———. " 'My Christ' in *Dutchman*," *College Language Association Journal* 15 (1971–72): 54–58. Examines Christian archetypes in the play.

BIGSBY, C. W. E. *Confrontation and Commitment: A Study of Contemporary American Drama 1959–1966*. Columbia: University of Missouri Press, 1967. Reduces Baraka's dramas to "revenge fantasies" that are inspired by an "obsession" with racial themes.

———. *Dada and Surrealism*. London: Methuen, 1972. A useful overview of the kind of literary movements that influence Baraka's early work.

BRADY, OWEN E. "Baraka's *Experimental Death Unit # 1*: Plan for (R)evolution," *Negro American Literature Forum* 9:2 (Summer 1975): 59–61. Views the play as evidence of Baraka's belief in the possibilities of human evolution from moral decadence to a new moral order.

BRECHT, STEFAN. "LeRoi Jones' *Slave Ship*," *Drama Review* 14:2 (Winter 1970): 212–19. Analyzes the imagist structure of the play and its appeal to a black audience.

BROWN, LLOYD W. "Comic Strip Heroes: LeRoi Jones and the Myth of American Innocence," *Journal of Popular Culture* 3 (Fall 1969): 191–204. Examines the significance of popular myths and cultural archetypes in Baraka's earlier poetry.

———. "The Cultural Revolution in Black Theatre," *Negro American Literature Forum* 8 (Spring 1974): 159–74. Includes a survey of revolutionary themes in Baraka's drama.

———. "High and Crazy Niggers: Anti-Rationalism in LeRoi Jones," *Journal of Ethnic Studies* 2:1 (Spring 1974). Discusses Baraka's attack on narrow forms of rationalism in Western culture.

———. "Jones (Baraka) and His Literary Heritage in *The System of Dante's Hell*," *Obsidian* 1 (Spring 1975): 5–17. Western literary influences in Baraka's novel.

_____. "LeRoi Jones as Novelist: Theme and Structure in *The System of Dante's Hell*," *Negro American Literature Forum* 7:4 (Winter 1973): 132–42. A survey of major themes and narrative techniques in the novel.

BURFORD, W. W. "LeRoi Jones: From Existentialism to Apostle of Black Nationalism," *Players* 47 (December 1972): 60–64. Traces evolution of Baraka's themes from an early nonracial emphasis to the racial perspectives of the later works.

COLEMAN, LARRY G. "LeRoi Jones' *Tales*: Sketches of the Artist as a Young Man Moving toward a Blacker Art," *Black Lines* 1:2 (Winter 1970): 17–26. A useful, pioneering study of Baraka's short stories. Evaluates the significance of the stories in Baraka's general development as a writer.

COSTELLO, DONALD P. "Black Man as Victim," *Commonweal* 88 (June 28, 1968): 436–40. Attacks Baraka's plays as "hate-ridden" works.

CRUSE, HAROLD. *The Crisis of the Negro Intellectual.* New York: William Morrow, 1967. Questions the soundness of the black nationalist criteria espoused by Baraka and others.

ELLISON, RALPH. *Shadow and Act.* New York: New American Library, 1966. Includes a generally unsympathetic review of Baraka's *Blues People*.

FISCHER, WILLIAM C. "The Pre-Revolutionary Writings of Imamu Amiri Baraka," *Massachusetts Review* 14 (Spring 1973): 259–305. An excellent survey of Baraka's early works, with an emphasis on his ethnic growth as a writer.

GAYLE, ADDISON, JR., *The Black Aesthetic.* New York: Doubleday, 1971. Representative essays on the black aesthetic that are comparable with Baraka's perception of the subject.

HAGOPIAN, JOHN V. "Another Ride on Jones's Subway," *College Language Association Journal* 21 (December 1977): 269–74. Examines the influence of the legend of the Flying Dutchman in Baraka's *Dutchman*.

HEGEL, GEORG W. F. *Aesthetics: Lectures on Fine Art.* Translated T. M. Knox. Oxford: Clarendon Press, 1975. One of the major Western influences in Baraka's early work, particularly on his interest in the relationship between art and feeling.

JACKSON, ESTHER M. "LeRoi Jones (Imamu Amiri Baraka): Form and the Progression of Consciousness," *College Language Association Journal* 17 (September 1973): 33–56. Traces the influence of German philosophers and American transcendentalists in *The System of Dante's Hell*.

JACOBUS, LEE. "Imamu Amiri Baraka: The Quest for Moral Order," in *Modern Black Poets*, ed. Donald B. Gibson. Englewood Cliffs, N.J.: Prentice-Hall, 1973, pp. 112–26. A useful study of the influence of Western writers, especially Eliot, on Baraka's poetry.

KLINKOWITZ, JEROME. "LeRoi Jones (Imamu Amiri Baraka): *Dutchman* as Drama," *Negro American Literature Forum* 7:4 (Winter 1973): 123–26. The study of black identity in Baraka's play.

_____. *Literary Disruptions: The Making of a Post-Contemporary Amer-*

ican Fiction. Urbana: University of Illinois, 1975. Includes references to Baraka's fiction.

KNOX, GEORGE. "The Mythology of LeRoi Jones' *Dutchman,*" in *Intercul-ture,* ed. Sy M. Khan. Vienna: Braumuller, 1975, pp. 243–51. Studies the role of myth in the play's themes.

LEDERER, RICHARD. "The Language of LeRoi Jones' *The Slave,*" *Studies in Black Literature* 4:1 (Spring 1973): 14–16. Defends the play's violent language as a functional element in Baraka's "theater of violence."

LINDBERG, JOHN. "*Dutchman* and *The Slave:* Comparisons in Revolution," *Black Academy Review* 2:1–2 (Spring-Summer 1971): 101–108. The "race war" theme in Baraka's plays.

LITTLEJOHN, DAVID. *Black on White: A Critical Survey of Writing by American Negroes.* New York: Viking, 1966. Representative of earlier, generally hostile responses to Baraka's work.

MARGOLIES, EDWARD. *Native Sons: A Critical Study of Twentieth-Century Negro American Authors.* Philadelphia: Lippincott, 1968. Includes an abusive rather than informative section on Baraka.

MENCHISE, DON M. "LeRoi Jones and a Case of Shifting Identities," *College Language Association Journal* 20 (1976–77): 232–34. Sees Baraka's career simply as a series of erratic shifts and changes.

MILLER, JEANNE-MARIE A. "The Plays of LeRoi Jones," *College Language Association Journal* 14 (1970–71): 331–39. Argues that Baraka's plays fulfill his own criterion that theater should advocate social change.

MUNRO, C. LYNN. "LeRoi Jones: A Man in Transition," *College Language Association Journal* 17 (September 1973): 57–78. Discusses some of the relationships between Dante's *Inferno* and Baraka's *System of Dante's Hell.*

NELSON, HUGHES. "LeRoi Jones' *Dutchman*: A Brief Ride on a Doomed Ship," *Educational Theater Journal* 20 (1968): 53–59. A survey of major themes in the play.

O'BRIEN, JOHN. *Interviews with Black Writers.* New York: Liveright, 1973. Includes comments on the influence of jazz on Baraka's writings.

PEAVY, CHARLES D. "Myth, Magic and Manhood in LeRoi Jones' *Madheart,*" *Studies in Black Literature* 1:2 (Summer 1970): 12–20. Analyzes the racial types and the use of biblical myth in Baraka's revolutionary drama.

PENNINGTON-JONES, PAULETTE, "From Brother LeRoi Jones through *The System of Dante's Hell* to Imamu Ameer Baraka," *Journal of Black Studies* 4 (December 1973): 195–214. Traces major changes in Baraka's ethnic views as they are reflected in his writing.

PHILLIPS, LOUIS. "LeRoi Jones and Contemporary Black Drama," in *The Black American Writer.* C. W. E. Bigsby, ed. Deland, Fla.: Everett/Edwards, 1969, II, 203–17. Discusses the symbolic significance of violence in Baraka's early plays.

PRIMEAU, RONALD. "Imagination as Moral Bulwark and Creative Energy in

Richard Wright's *Black Boy* and LeRoi Jones' *Home*," *Studies in Black Literature* 3:2 (Summer 1972): 12–18. Includes discussion of Baraka's perception of the black writer's role.

RICE, JULIAN C. "LeRoi Jones' *Dutchman*: A Reading," *Contemporary Literature* 12 (1971): 42–59. Links play with Baraka's analysis of black music in *Blues People*.

SCHORER, MARK. "Technique as Discovery," *Hudson Review* 1 (1948): 67–87. A definitive statement on the relationship between form and theme in prose fiction, one that is very useful in the study of Baraka's *System of Dante's Hell*.

TAYLOR, CLYDE. "Baraka as Poet," in *Modern Black Poets*. Donald B. Gibson, ed. Englewood Cliffs, N.J.: Prentice-Hall, 1973, pp. 127–34. A solid survey of major trends in Baraka's development as poet.

TAYLOR, WILLIAM P. "The Fall of Man Theme in Imamu Amiri Baraka's (LeRoi Jones') *Dutchman*," *Negro American Literature Forum* 7:4 (Winter 1973): 127–30. Examines Christian typology in the play.

TENER, ROBERT L. "The Corrupted Warrior Heroes: Amiri Baraka's *The Toilet*," *Modern Drama* 17 (June 1974): 207–15. Discusses the play as an analysis of the impact of (white) myths of heroism on blacks.

———. "Role Playing as a Dutchman," *Studies in Black Literature* 3:3 (Fall 1972): 17–21. Traces parallels between the play's archetypal roles and the kinds of role-playing that are current in America's racial relationships.

WEISGRAM, DIANNE H. "LeRoi Jones' *Dutchman*: Inter-racial Ritual of Sexual Violence," *American Imago* 29 (Fall 1972): 215–32. A turgid "psychological reading of the play in order to explain how its activation of fundamental psychological conflicts enhances its political impact."

WILLIAMS, SHERLEY ANNE. *Give Birth to Brightness: A Thematic Study in Neo-Black Literature*. New York: Dial Press, 1972. Includes remarks on Baraka's works.

WILLIS, ROBERT J. "Anger and the Contemporary Black Theatre," *Negro American Literature Forum* 8:2 (Summer 1974): 213–15. Sees Baraka's militancy as the reflection of a major and continuing tradition in black theater.

WITHERINGTON, PAUL. "Exorcism and Baptism in LeRoi Jones' *The Toilet*," *Modern Drama* 15 (Summer 1972): 159–63. A neo-Freudian reading of the play as an "archetypal struggle" to free the self from the "pre-adolescent maternal community."

ZATLIN, LINDA G. "Paying His Dues: Ritual in LeRoi Jones' Early Dramas," *Obsidian* 2:1 (Spring 1976): 21–31. Argues that Baraka criticizes society by incorporating its failing rituals into his plays.

Index

179